D0710557

FROM MISSION
TO METROPOLIS

FROM MISSION TO METROPOLIS

Cupeño Indian Women
in Los Angeles

By Diana Meyers Bahr

University of Oklahoma Press : Norman and London

This book is published with the generous assistance of Edith Gaylord Harper.

Library of Congress Cataloging-in-Publication Data

Bahr, Diana Meyers, 1930–
    From mission to metropolis : Cupeñeo Indian
women in Los Angeles / by Diana Meyers Bahr.
       p.   cm.
    Includes bibliographical references (p.   ) and
index.
    ISBN 0-8061-2549-7 (alk. paper)
    1. Cupeño Indians—Women. 2. Cupeño In-
dians—Biography. 3. Cupeño Indians—Ethnic
identity. I. Title.
E99.C94B35 1993
305.48'8974—dc20   93-13176
                                                   CIP

Text design by Cathy Imboden.

To Anna, Patricia, and Tracie,
who, with love and generosity,
have shared their life histories with me.
They carry on the tradition of storytellers,
who go back to *Mulu'Wetam*, the first people,
and through whom Cupeño culture has endured.

CONTENTS

C O N T E N T S
viii

ILLUSTRATIONS

ACKNOWLEDGMENTS

I would like to express my gratitude to the following people who shared the experience of creating this work with me in myriad helpful, generous, and loving ways. A number of these people were my mentors at UCLA. Kenneth Lincoln showed me the "good red road" of American Indian studies and stayed with me step by step along this challenging and rewarding path. His impressive knowledge and his creative spirit permeate this work. Norris C. Hundley was discriminating, encouraging, and caring. I am deeply thankful for Charlotte Heth's encouragement and support, which have been consistent from the first day I met her. Not only has Eric Monkkonen been my friend and ally since the beginning of my career at UCLA, but his keen interest and wide-ranging knowledge have greatly contributed to this work. I will always be grateful to Dale Trelevan, who introduced me to oral history and encouraged and advised me throughout the creation of the life histories of the Dawn family. Robert A. Georges presented the scholarly literature of folklore studies and anthropology with a depth and breadth that proved to be an invaluable foundation for my work. I am very grateful for the strength and conviction of Paul Kroskrity. Vee Salabiye, librarian in the American Indian Studies Center, rescued me repeatedly with her detective talents, including finding an important citation for me by recognizing the handwriting of the source. My heartfelt thanks go to Joan Weibel-Orlando, University of Southern California, for her careful and sensitive reading of the manuscript.

I am deeply thankful for the love and support of Gary Meyers, Timothy Meyers, Christopher Meyers, and Pat Holmes. To my husband, Ehrhard "Ted" Bahr, goes my most appreciative recognition. No one has shared this journey with me as he has.

FROM MISSION
TO METROPOLIS

Genealogical Chart

Anna May Smith m. Steven Helm

Belva May Helm m. Charles King

Anna May King —— (1st) m. George Ryan   Charles King, Jr.

Patricia Ann Ryan (1st) m. Tony Condello

Tracie Ann Condello

(2nd) m. James Nichols

(2nd) m. Harold Dean Dawn

Steven Dawn

CHAPTER 1

Introduction

Belonging was a matter of deciding to.

—Lipshaw Morrissey,
in Love Medicine *by Louise Erdrich*

As one drives along Santa Fe Avenue through the light-industrial Huntington Park area of Los Angeles, the dominance of the Hispanic population is vividly evident. Restaurants named El Ranchito or Mariscos Mazatlan are more numerous than McDonald's or Wendy's. The *carnicerías* sell *sólo carne fresca* and La Perla Market advertises *productos Mexicanos*. In Santa Fe Plaza, a mini-mall near Santa Fe and Gage avenues, is a satellite office of the U.S. Department of Justice, Immigration, and Naturalization Service. Two doors away is a storefront private immigration agency with a sign proclaiming, *"Proceso para residencia permanente."*

Tucked into a corner one block southeast of the intersection of Santa Fe and Gage avenues is an attractive residential street, where ice cream vendors, virtually no longer seen elsewhere in metropolitan Los Angeles, still serenade the working-class neighborhood with their musical trucks. In the middle of the block, an extraordinarily neat bungalow-style house, newly stuccoed in a rich beige, is set off by a black wrought-iron fence, which encloses the well-manicured front yard. Behind this house sits a smaller version, just as neat and well kept. Anna, a red-haired, green-eyed, vivacious grandmother, lives in the front house, which is the gathering place for all family activities, varying from daily get-togethers to festive holiday celebrations. In the back house live her daughter, Patricia (Pat), also red-haired and green-eyed but with a complexion much fairer than that of her mother, and Pat's daughter, Tracie, a tall, striking blond with blue-green eyes. Most observers would never guess that these women are members of a small California Mission Indian tribe, the Cupeño, who probably numbered between 500 and 750 persons at the time of contact with Europeans in 1795 and who presently have an estimated population of only 150 people.[1]

Three of these 150 persons have narrated this life history of their urban Cupeño family. The oldest is Anna May Dawn, sixty-six, a widow.[2] She is the mother of the second-oldest interviewee, Patricia Ann (Pat) Ryan, forty-nine, who is the divorced mother of the youngest narrator, Tracie Ann Condello, who is twenty-three and single. In this family history, I hope to convey to the reader what it means to be an urban American Indian woman experiencing cultural change, how urban Indian women feel and think about this change, and how they express their feelings and thinking. The three urban Indian women in this study manifest forms of tribal beliefs in ways that reveal the emergence over time of new forms of ethnicity.

The women of the Dawn family are presented here not in a chronological biography, but in an anthropological life history situated within a historical context. Unlike autobiography or biography, with which it is often grouped, life history is a collaboration between both the researcher and the subject.[3]

American Indian life history has been predominantly a collaborative form that mirrors the convergence of two cultures, that of the Indian whose life is being recorded and that of the white recorder-historian. Because the collaboration relies heavily on spoken narration, the terms *oral history* and *life history* are often used interchangeably. However, I do not consider the terms synonymous. As oral historian Jeff Todd Titon has pointed out, the overriding concern of oral history is factual accuracy.[4] Life history also has a time depth, relating local history from the view of indigenous narrators. Although life history may well be accurate, it is concerned more with presenting the perceptions of the narrators than with documenting historical veracity.[5]

The reader will come to know Anna, Patricia, and Tracie not through descriptions of their life-styles, but in a manner similar to the way in which I came to know them—bit by bit, through their expressed emotions and thoughts recorded during six months of interviews, November 1988 through May 1989, augmented by continuing conversations. To assist the reader in integrating these narrative mosaics, I have presented, in chapter 2, a chronological history of the lives of the family members. Three major themes recur dramatically in the interviews: (1) perceptions of family versus individuality; (2) beneficence; and (3) the metaphysical realm. These themes, which emerge as the sinews that help keep the family intact in the face of change, may help illuminate cultural change in urban Indian families. We are in danger of losing knowledge of the rich experiences of Indians because of widespread ignorance. Historian Hazel W. Hertzberg's contention that "sympathy for the Indian is not the same as knowledge of him—and knowledge is not keeping pace" is especially pertinent to the urban Indian woman.[6]

Although urban Indians constitute more than 50 percent of the North American native population, Indians in the city are often considered the invisible minority. The Cupeño, who live in relative obscurity on reservations in southern Riverside and northern San Diego counties, are totally obscure as an ethnic group in the city of Los Angeles. Moreover, the lack of literature on urban Indian women leaves many unanswered questions.[7] We have much to learn about Indian women in the city: the problems unique to this population, the details of their daily lives, their personal relationships, and the factors that contribute to persistence or change in their awareness of being Indian.[8]

Early in the interviews of Anna, Patricia, and Tracie, I recognized differences in the degree to which they perceive themselves as Indian. Anna became aware that she was Indian when she was around six or seven years old (1–9).[9] She remembers that when playing cowboys and Indians, she always wanted to be the Indian and became very distressed when the other children protested: "Get outta here. You're not an Indian!" (1–10). She came to her grandmother one day crying and asked: "How come the kids make fun of the Indians? And they tell me I'm not an Indian?" (1–10). Anna's maternal grandmother, Anna Lawson Helm, who had a powerful influence on her, responded: "Don't pay any attention to 'em. They don't know. They probably never even seen any [Indians]." Anna recalls, "That's what she'd always tell me: 'Your heritage is Indian'" (1–10). Anna identifies so strongly as Indian that she regrets not being able to attend a school exclusively for Indians, as did her grandmother, who attended Carlisle Indian Industrial School in Pennsylvania.

Patricia was even younger when she became aware that she was Indian; her maternal grandmother, Belva May Helm King, took her to powwows and fiestas on the reservations. "My grandmother would take me when I was knee high. And I remember a lot of those" (2—14). She especially remembers the men sitting around a campfire and talking about some of the negative aspects of being Indian, such as the poverty and the problem with alcohol. "It's mostly the poverty level that they couldn't get beyond. They didn't have much education. . . . If they completed grammar school it was a miracle" (2–15). Recognition of these negative aspects was coupled with an awareness that the women did not participate in these discussions. "The women weren't allowed to sit around the campfire. It was only the men" (2–17).

This awareness apparently generated a rebellion in Patricia against certain aspects of her Indian heritage. "If I had been older, I'd probably be sitting with the men. . . . They probably would have made a scene. But I'm very outgoing" (2–17). Her ambivalent feelings about being Indian led her into conflict with her grandmother, who wanted Pat to marry an Indian. "Why," she asked her grandmother, "do you want me to be married to an Indian man and walk behind him?" (2–20). Nevertheless, Pat is proud of her Indian heritage. She devoted considerable time and energy to the Indian Free Clinic in Huntington Park and greatly regrets its closing.

Tracie's identification as an Indian is strongly tied to her love for her grandmother. Regarding depictions of Indians as violent, she protests: "That's not right. Indians aren't like that" (8–5). When asked what Indians are like, she responds: "Indians are, I guess, like my grandma. . . . She's not violent" (8–5). Tracie recalls becoming aware, when she was about six or seven, of family members talking about being Indian. She did not talk to anyone about her Indian heritage, however, until she was eighteen years old and noticed her grandmother's growing pan-Indian art collection, which evidently stimulated Tracie's curiosity (8–8). When asked if she would be interested in learning more about her Indian background, she responds: "To tell you the truth, I really would. [I would like to] learn about how my family was" (8–37).

Because of these varied responses, the question "Who is an Indian?" became primary in this study. A review of the literature reveals that a definition of Indian ethnicity is complex and often open-ended.[10]

WHO IS AN INDIAN?

Each ethnic group in the United States has been confronted with the need to define itself and its place in American society. Indians, however, have faced the question of their relationship to the wider society for a longer time than any other group. In seeking ways to define themselves as Americans, Indians have confronted a range of dilemmas: they have been regarded as a separate race; the reservation has been their ghetto; their human rights have been ignored; their poverty has been endemic; and their education has been unrelated to their cultures.[11]

But what do people mean when they refer to "Indian culture"? The question "Who is an Indian?" is laden with difficulty and uncertainty.[12] Some scholars go so far as to declare that it may be impossible to assert definitively who is an Indian in the United States today.[13] This phenomenon is further complicated by the fact that virtually all Indian history has been written from a non-Indian bias. The history of the white image of the Indian demonstrates that American Indians have consistently been perceived as a separate other. This bias has been explored by a number of scholars, notably Robert F. Berkhofer, Jr., in *The White Man's Indian.* "Whether evaluated as noble or ignoble, whether seen as exotic or degraded, the Indian as an image was always alien to the White."[14] Raymond W. Stedman believes that each new white generation has reinvented the Indian in the image of its own era.[15]

Despite this periodic reinvention, Berkhofer has identified three persistent themes evident throughout the history of the white interpretation of Indians: (1) generalizing from one tribe to all Indians; (2) conceiving of Indians in terms of their deficiencies, as perceived by whites; and (3) using moral evaluations of native life-styles as descriptions of Indians.[16] Considerable scholarly literature has been devoted to exploring the persistent perception that there could be a place for Indians in American society only if they became "white." Several scholars have noted that in response to the pressure to assimilate, Indians have been remarkably adaptive.[17] In ironic contrast to the pressure to assimilate, there remains a persistent danger of stereotyping, due in large measure to the conflation of all Indians into *the* Indian. Images of American Indians in films reveal that mass arts prefer the allegorical and portray surfaces and types rather than essences and individuals.[18]

Pat angrily remembers seeing drunken Indians portrayed in films. "They don't show very many white people standing up against a wall with a bottle in their hand. It's always an Indian" (2–46). Tracie was not aware of the "drunken Indian" cliché, a clear indication of change over time. When I asked her how she felt about such a stereotype, she responded very personally: "My grandmother's an Indian. She don't get drunk. My mom's an Indian. She don't get drunk. My [great-great]-grandfather never touched a drink in his life" (10–20).

Indians continue to be labeled in inaccurate, misleading, static, and derogatory terms, not only in the media but also in educational materials.[19] Pat Ryan remembers negative depictions in her school textbooks. "They never talk about battles [Indians] won. They always talked about the massacres" (4–10). "Indians were portrayed as murderers, drunkards, thieves. . . . They don't talk about the good things [Indians have] done" (4–11).

While recognizing stereotypes, complexities, and ambiguities, C. Matthew Snipp and James L. Simmons, among others, have identified six basic ways by which Indianness is defined: (1) legal definitions, primarily enrollment in a recognized tribe; (2) self-declaration, used in the U.S. census; (3) recognition by an Indian community; (4) recognition by non-Indians; (5) biological definition, usually specified by blood quantum; and (6) cultural definitions, as defined by both Indians and whites.[20] How each member of the Dawn family conforms to each of these definitions is a significant avenue for exploring the change in and persistence of Indianness in this family.

For legal definition, ethnicity is confirmed by the tribe and by the federal government. Anna and Patricia are enrolled on the Cupeño tribal register; Tracie is not. Having been told previously that enrollment had a cutoff date that precluded Tracie's registration, they appear unsure of both the date and the reason for it. It is likely that the cutoff date they refer to is that of May 24, 1950, the last date of birth allowed for inscription on the "Great Roll" of California Indians, compiled by the Bureau of Indian Affairs. A series of "Great Rolls," begun in the 1920s, was intended to document the name of every California Indian who qualified for a special financial subvention by the U.S. government. As a result of a settlement of native land claims, a new roll was begun in 1970.[21] Anna and Patricia are currently attempting, with the assistance of Anna's cousin, who has closer contacts with the tribal office, to get Tracie enrolled.

Self-declaration involves the relationship of the individual to the larger society. Anna declares herself American Indian for census data, as does Patricia, despite her Irish heritage. Tracie, when asked how she would identify herself, responded, "Indian, Irish, and Italian." When asked which she would select if she had to choose one ethnic identity for census purposes, she responded, "Indian." When asked why, she replied, "Because of my grandmother; it's important to my grandmother."[22]

Another way to define Indianness is recognition by an Indian community. As a family, all three women are unofficially recognized by the Mission Indian communities of Pala, Pechanga, Mesa Verde, Santa Ysabel, Rincon, and possibly others. These communities, which include Cupeño, Cahuilla, and Luiseño, are small enough to allow for recognition of family names, such as that of Anna's grandfather, Steve Helm. Pat remembers playing with Indian kids during visits to the reservations. "I was very fair [complexioned] . . . and I guess a lot of 'em didn't think that I was Indian until my grandmother said [I was]" (2–43). During a visit to the area as an adult, however, she walked into a bar seeking directions to her uncle's place. "The bartender looked at me and said, 'You're Steve Helm's [great-]granddaughter'" (2–44). Moreover, the Dawns have matching T-shirts enscribed with "Pala Indian Reservation." Whenever they wear the shirts to a powwow away from Pala, people inevitably come up to them and say things like "I went to school with your cousin," or "I knew your aunt and uncle."

Recognition by non-Indians also defines Indianness. In this category one can clearly discern change over time in the Dawn family. Whites may perceive Anna's physical Indianness despite her red hair. When she is sometimes mistaken for Mexican, she becomes hostile. A woman in a supermarket spoke to her in Spanish, and Anna responded: "For your information, I don't speak that damn Mexican. . . . I happen to be an Indian" (1–7). Pat, with her red hair and green eyes and fair complexion, is virtually never initially thought of as being Indian, a misperception that she aggressively corrects. Even the children of her second husband, James Nichols, thought for a short time that the Dawn family was Mexican. "My mother is dark," Pat explains. "My brother is dark. And I was the light one." She instructed these stepchildren: "No, we're not Mexican. We're Indians. Not from India but from the United States." Pat persisted in educating them until "they accepted it" (4–22). Tracie, also fair-complexioned, is not perceived as Indian. She neither is aggressive about her ethnic identity nor denies it. She claims that it does not matter to her that she is not registered as a California Indian. "To me, I am one. Because I have Indian blood in me and my family is Indian, and I'm proud to be an Indian" (10–38).

Biological definition is a situation with both legal and personal aspects. By blood quantum, Anna claims to be full-blooded American Indian; Patricia claims to be half-Indian and Tracie one-quarter.[23]

Cultural definitions, which can be determined by myriad situations, are much more ambiguous and complex. What emerges from the interviews is these urban Indians' dramatic insistence on retaining their ethnic identity. In *The Names*, N. Scott Momaday wrote about the time that his mother, a one-eighth-blood Cherokee, began to see herself as an Indian, when she was sixteen years old. "That dim native heritage became a fascination for her. . . . She imagined who she was. This act of imagination was, I believe, among the most important events of my mother's early life, as later the same essential act was to be among the most important of my own."[24] In *Love Medicine*, a novel about the Turtle Mountain band of Chippewa Indians in North Dakota, Louise Erdrich dramatized that belonging very often *is* a matter of deciding to. Anna relates that her grandfather was always proud to be an Indian, but his brother was not. Her great-uncle would say: "Why bother with saying you're an Indian. You don't get any reward for it" (3–26). Anna remembers, though, that later in life the great-uncle and his family "decided they gonna be Indian." She seems puzzled by this history. "But until then, they just never wanted anybody to know. Why, I don't know" (3–28).

This persistence in ethnic identification defies the expectations of non-Indians. The imminent disappearance of the American Indian has been predicted since contact. The facts, however, reveal that Indians have endured biologically, with a steady increase in population since the turn of the century, and perhaps even more significantly, that they have endured culturally. This endurance may be due in part to a high degree of diversity, which engenders different senses of identity. Diversity is especially apparent among urban Indians.

INDIANS IN THE CITY

Although scholars and the general public alike observe that Indian cultures are most obviously preserved on the reservations, demographic data reveal that 62 percent of contemporary American Indians live in urban areas.[25] Los Angeles County has an Indian population of 45,508, according to the 1990 census, but leaders of the Los Angeles Indian community claim this figure is a gross undercount, with the estimated total being between 75,000 and 100,000.[26] Whichever figure one accepts, Los Angeles is recognized as the largest urban center of American Indians in the United States. UCLA scholar Kenneth Lincoln has pointed out that Indians, who have moved or been "removed" to villages, towns, and cities, were peoples who were "earlier defined by geographics, histories, genetics, and cultures indigeneous over centuries." He wrote, "They bring this Indianness with them into the city, redefining themselves."[27]

Around 1920, Anna's grandparents moved to Los Angeles from the Mesa Grande area in southern Riverside County. "There were opportunities. There were more jobs here for my grandfather" (1–2). He worked primarily as a butcher, as he had on the ranch near Mesa Grande. Years later Anna's divorced mother became skillful at obtaining urban employment. "She worked in the bakery, . . . worked for doctors. . . . She even took care of Bing Crosby's kids" (1–3). Although redefinition of Indian identity in the city requires the capacity to adapt, this adaptation does not necessarily make one less

Indian.[28] "Wipe your Indian hands on your Levi jeans," declares George C. Longfish, Iroquois-Seneca-Tuscaora artist, "get into your Toyota pick-up. Throw in a tape of Mozart, Led Zeppelin or ceremonial Sioux songs; then throw your head back and laugh—you are a survivor of a colonized people. Paint what you see, sculpt what you feel, and stay amused."[29]

Longfish hints at a crucial phenomenon in urban Indian redefinition, that of pan-Indianism, which is often perceived as the diffusion from tribe to tribe of traits that originated in the nineteenth-century culture of the Plains Indians. A number of scholars have recognized, however, that pan-Indianism has come to mean a broadening awareness of Indianness in contrast to white culture.[30] John A. Price asserts that the majority of Indians in Los Angeles "clearly are ideologically and emotionally affiliated with pan-Indianism." Moreover, Price has found that the length of time in the city and the degree of disintegration of tribal culture correlate with the level of urban assimilation.[31]

Thus, it is no surprise that Anna Dawn manifests more colorfully than does Pat or Tracie an affiliation with pan-Indianism. To her large pan-Indian art collection, Anna longs to add a tepee, a totem pole, and a Plains Indian headdress, not one of which is indigenous to the Cupeño. "I know it's stupid," she says, "but I would like to put up a tepee. . . . I want to do that so bad" (3–46). When asked why she wants to have a totem pole, she responds: "Well, I think they're beautiful, . . . a heritage, you know" (5–1). She insists that the headdress have real eagle feathers. "I don't want those turkey feathers" (5–2). The motivating dynamic of urban pan-Indianism has been the desire of American Indians to retain an Indian identity in the city.[32] Price believes that pan-Indianism not only becomes an additional dimension to ethnic identity but also is sometimes a substitute for tribal affiliation.[33] Price's observation is clearly evident in the pan-Indian affiliations of Anna, Pat, and Tracie.

All three women favor the idea of establishing a pan-Indian cultural center in Los Angeles. "I would support it wholeheartedly," says Pat (4–39). When asked what she would like to do in such a center, she responds: "Talk about customs, dress. I think the women, their buckskin dresses were gorgeous. . . . And moccasins and stuff. And their headdresses. Just basically customs and the old ways" (4–39). When she declared that she would volunteer her time in a pan-Indian center, I ask: "And you would go there to be with other Indians? It wouldn't matter what tribe they were from?" (4–39). She responds: "No, because they're all the same. . . . To me they're all the same" (4–39). Tracie believes that the Indians "should be noticed. . . . They should have a club for Indians. Like the Elks Club" (10–24). When asked if she would participate in an Indian activist group, she responds with an answer that appears to be more closely tied to her love for and loyalty to her family than to a desire to associate with other Indians: "I would. I'd help out my grandma as much as I could and my mom" (10–25).

Anna criticizes factionalism among Indians. "I think it's good, long as you're an Indian, we should all be together" (9–25). "It is nice, regardless of what nation, I mean what tribe you're from, [to] get together and stay together" (9–27). Observing that Indians usually identify themselves by tribe, she says: "See, they don't [stay together] though. They start fighting amongst themselves about everything. And one tribe wants this, and the other tribe says, 'No, I want to take this for my tribe'" (9–27).

Tracie's affiliation is clearly with her family, rather than an Indian community. She says, "My family is Indian." Although they rarely identify themselves as Cupeño, Anna and Pat feel an affiliation with Mission Indians. I first met Anna and Pat in October 1988, at the Southwest Museum of Native Cultures of the Americas in Los Angeles. During a presentation on the Chumash Indians of California, the moderator asked if there were any Indians in the audience. Among the people who raised their hands was Patricia. Because I was looking for interview subjects, Indian women who had grown up in Los Angeles, I noted those who raised their hands. After the presentation, I approached Pat and asked if she had identified herself as an Indian. Her response was both positive and emphatic. When I asked if she had grown up in Los Angeles, she replied: "Yes, and this is my mother, who grew up in Los Angeles. And I have a daughter who grew up in Los Angeles." Then Anna added that the family had lived in the city for five generations. When they agreed to participate in my research, I asked them which tribe they were affiliated with, and they both responded: "Mission Indian." In a subsequent interview, Anna told me that the family had Cupeño heritage.

When she identifies herself as a Mission Indian, Anna sometimes elicits the question, "From California?" She responds: "Yeah. What's wrong with that? I'm proud to be a Mission Indian" (9–27). She believes that even Indians know very little about California Indians. "They very seldom meet a California Indian. I mean, born here in California" (9–27).

Pat seems almost militantly pan-Indian, believing that the most effective way to participate in a redefinition of Indian identity may be through politics. "The only time you see a lot of Indians are in Christmas parades [and similar] doings. And they talk about how great they were. *Were!*" (13–24). When asked what she thinks Indians should do now, she responds: "Stand up and be counted. . . . Stand there and say, 'This is the way it should be with us'" (13–25). Although Tracie appears to have no strong political inclinations, she thinks she might like to participate in an Indian political group. "It's my family background. I'm the third [living] generation and I would like to know" (10–38).

Anna manifests a more compelling need to participate in the redefinition of Indian identity. "I know it sounds kind of dumb, us being Indians . . . and I'm just now really . . . getting into it. 'Course I was always an Indian anyway. But it's like now . . . I want it so bad, you know" (12–41). She treasures her great-grandmother's few remaining handmade baskets, only one of which is in Anna's possession. She intends to ask her brother for the ones he has, because she believes they mean less to him than to her (12–2). Anna's mother, unable to learn basket weaving from Anna's grandmother because of the pressure to make a living in the city, later attempted her own redefinition by attending basket-weaving classes. "She wanted to [weave baskets] even up till the time she passed away," relates Anna. "That's what she wanted to do. Because she said that it's an art, . . . especially the pine needle. The pine needle baskets" (12–3).

To the question "Who is an Indian?" the Kiowa Pulitzer Prize–winning author N. Scott Momaday responds: "An Indian is an idea which a given man has of himself. And it is a moral idea, for it accounts for the way in which he reacts to other men and to the world in general. And that idea, in order to be realized completely, has to be expressed."[34] This recognition of the need to "tell," expressed by Momaday, is evident in the narrations of the Dawn family.

Although Tracie, at first, was intimidated by the interview process, the need to tell became stronger when she realized that the focus was on her relationships with members of her family. After the first interview, she remarked to Anna, "As soon as she asked what kind of influence Grandpa Dean had on me, it was o.k." For the remainder of the interviews, Tracie's willingness to participate was linked with her desire to tell about her family.

Anna, a charming storyteller, exhibited considerable delight in relating narratives. Yet she believes that Indians as a group do not know how to express themselves. "If they got something to say, they don't come out and say it. They hold it in. . . . They are the silent . . . group. . . . They're bashful" (9–49). Pat remembers hearing old tribal stories during her visits to Pala and Temecula, the traditional homes of the Cupeño, and would love to hear them again because she has forgotten them (13–37). All three women, but most strongly Anna and Pat, have repeatedly expressed gratitude to be able to tell their stories. When I informed them that there would be no remuneration for their participation in the study, Pat replied, "The chance to tell our story is all the payment we need."[35]

Anna complains about the lack of knowledge about contemporary urban Indian women.[36] Recalling that people have asked her if she lives in a tepee, she remarks, "Now, that is dumb" (9–7). She relates an experience she had with a girl friend's mother who wanted to meet a "real live Indian." "Well, she was asking me what I ate, and I said, 'Well, I eat just like anybody else.' . . . And she said, 'What do you really eat?' I says, 'I eat anything.' I don't know what she expected. . . . I don't know what was with the corn, but she asked me a dozen times if I ate corn" (9–8).

When told that non-Indians are astonished to learn that there are over forty-five thousand Indians in Los Angeles, Tracie counters: "Well, they're not going to run out in their headdresses and moccasins" (8–38). Expressing her belief that people cannot learn about contemporary Indians from museum exhibits, Pat advises: "Visiting. Seeing. The real life stuff . . . going downtown and seeing them live in a shack" (13–2).

METHODOLOGY

"Ethnography is a hybrid textual activity," states history of consciousness scholar James Clifford.[37] Such diverse fields as sociology, psychology, history, political science, anthropology, and literature have utilized life history as a methodological base. There has recently been a renewed interest in the use of life history in qualitative research.[38] Until recently, however, life histories have received little attention as a method for organizing data, except perhaps in culture and personality studies in social psychology.

Oral historian Geyla Frank explains this lack of attention by pointing out a paradox inherent in life-history research: the use of life history for research demands analysis and abstraction, yet the self-evidence of the life-history document makes it difficult to consider it a scientific model of the subject's life.[39] Although the data was not used to construct a scientific model of the lives of the Dawn women, the findings that emerged from the interviews became the organizing principle for my study. The themes of family versus individuality, beneficence, and metaphysics are the sinews that bind not only the Dawn family members but also the study based on them.

To facilitate the discussions of these themes, I have adopted the concept of *mentalité* as perceived by Jacques LeGoff.[40] Mentalité, the set of perceptions that exist in the mind and form the foundation for thoughts, feelings, and actions, is seen by LeGoff as having a "historical lag." This lag is created by the slow adaptation to change by mentalité. Lowell Bean makes a similar assumption. "A model of a culture can persist through time in the minds of the people, and . . . it is accurate in a broad sense . . . because an ideal model exists at an implicit level in the minds of the members of the culture."[41] Is there a historical lag in mentalité evident in the narrations of the Dawn women? The narrations indicate that there is.

Since mentalité is characterized by nuance and flux, the task of the researcher is to determine where mentalité undergoes change. This task requires an awareness not only of continuities but also of disappearances and discontinuities. The continuities and discontinuities revealed in the narrations indicate that the Dawn family appears to exemplify the type of urban population in which pan-Indian identification is evident and in which more than one cultural identity is maintained.[42]

Maintaining multiple cultural identities may be strongly affected by the decision of whom to marry.[43] Anna's first husband and Pat's biological father, George Ryan, was Irish. Anna believes, but has no documentation, that her second husband, Dean Dawn, who is the father of her son, Steven, was Indian, from a tribe in Missouri. Anna states that she would have liked for her children to marry Indians to ensure that tribal traditions do not disappear. "I feel they should marry into their own race" (3–19).

Pat expresses ambivalent feelings about marrying an Indian. Having perceived as a child and as a teenager that women on the reservations were sub-servient to the men, she questions: "They [the men] walk in front and I have to walk behind? No. I walk beside him. Or in front of him, but never behind him" (2–17). In contrast, she was uncomfortable when, while married to the Italian Tony Condello, she attended a meeting during which an Indian spoke out against intermarriage. "It kind of both-ered me. . . . If I had married an Indian, she [Tracie] would have been more [Indian] because of my blood ties and his blood ties. She would have been more. More than what she is now" (2–19). Although she herself has doubts about marrying an Indian, Pat states that she would like Tracie to marry an Indian. "Because it would make the blood ties stronger. For her child" (2–35). This wish is ex-pressed, however, with stipulations: as long as he is "modern" and does not believe that "a man's place is at the head of the table and a woman's place is at the end" (2–35).

Tracie recognizes that the culture of the Cupeño could disappear with her generation, but when asked about marrying an Indian, she responds: "I really don't know. . . . I don't know what the advan-tages are." Nor does she perceive disadvantages in marrying an Indian (11–47).

Intermarriage is only one aspect of the potential for change in the mentalité of urban Indians. Schol-ar James H. Stewart has constructed a model that incorporates the possible spectrum of change in urban Indians. Emphasizing that his model repre-sents variable processes and not discrete condi-tions, Stewart categorizes the factors influencing acculturation and assimilation into five major areas: (1) reservation factors; (2) conditions in the city; (3) primary relationships; (4) power and socioeco-nomic factors; and (5) racial factors.[44] Although I recognize the importance of all five categories of factors influencing acculturation and assimilation, I have incorporated in my study only the area of primary relationships. This decision is based on my conviction, substantiated by Stewart, that these relationships assume a saliency that provides a strong base for cultural persistence.

In "Who Is Your Mother?," Paula Gunn Allen, Laguna Pueblo author and scholar, discusses the belief held by "all American Indian Nations" that kinship is the root of individual and cultural identity. Kinship, especially matrilineal, defines the individual's "universal web . . . in each of its dimensions: cultural, spiritual, personal, and historical."[45] Although the same perception is strongest in the mentalité of Tracie, all three Dawn women look at their own family's traditions to define Indianness. The importance of family relationships is dramatically manifested in the narrations.

"I really enjoyed my mother," says Anna. "And we got along real, real good together" (2–1, 2). She believes that her relationship with Pat is just as strong as her own with her mother and that her ties with Tracie are as strong as Anna's were with her own grandmother. Regarding her daughter, Anna says: "We're very close. I mean really, we're like sisters. . . . I mean we sit down and talk, you know. All the time, about everything" (3–1). When Tracie was younger, she would tell Anna and her husband things that "maybe she'd be a little frightened to tell her mother, you know how kids do. But Tracie, that's one thing, we are very, very close" (3–2). Anna is very appreciative of the fact that when her father and her husband were both terminally ill and bedridden in her home, Tracie would be "right up here helping." Anna says, "She'd come in and . . . the first thing, say, 'Oh, Grandma, I'll do it'" (3–4).

The interaction among the family members shows their devotion to one another as clearly as do the comments during the interviews. At the beginning of one interview session with Pat, she asked Anna to make coffee. Anna teased, "Go ahead and make some if you like." Pat countered: "I can't make coffee today. I'm the star." Their mutual amusement with this exchange was both loving and accepting of one another. Pat emphatically states: "My family. My family needs me. I'm there. We have always been there. My daughter is the same way" (4–17). After her divorce from Tracie's father, Tony Condello, Pat's stepfather, Dean Dawn, helped raise Tracie. "He was the only male influence that she was around, because she was [with him and Anna] constantly. . . . My dad thought the world of my daughter and when he passed away, she says, 'I lost my dad.' She was very upset. She was hysterical" (4–23).

When asked who has had the most influence on her, Tracie corroborates Anna's and Pat's perceptions. "I have three people—that's my mom, my grandmother, and my grandfather. Those three people went out of their way to get things that I needed. And to teach me things." And she believes that the influence was equally divided among these three primary relationships (8–14). Tracie also has maintained close ties to steprelatives. "See, to me," she explains, "step doesn't mean anything. If you love the person, then you can accept them as your own" (11–26). This closeness is a pattern spanning generations in Tracie's family.

In tracing cultural persistence and change in the Dawn family over three generations, I have investigated the impact of personal relationships on three recurring themes. Although these three categories— family versus individuality, beneficence, and metaphysics — are not discrete and although some over-lapping occurs, the areas are conceptually distinct. The discussions of these aspects of mentalité are situated within historical contexts, which are presented in chapter 2.

I am particularly interested in chapter 3 in the persistence or change occurring over several generations in mentalité regarding family versus individuality. Since this feature of mentalité has the potential for alienation among family members, consistency in how family members regard individuality is, I believe, a vital cord that contributes to the strength of the Dawn family.

Although all three women have similar attitudes toward a number of ethical questions, one issue recurs dramatically throughout the interviews — that of beneficence. In chapter 4, I ask: Do the attitudes of Anna, Tracie, and Pat vary on the issue of helping others less fortunate than they? How does their interaction affect their thinking and behavior in this area?

In chapter 5, some of the most intriguing narrations are presented in the accounts, by all three women, of beliefs in and experiences with the metaphysical realm, including religion, dreams, visions, premonitions, and communications with loved ones who have died. I have attempted to locate the origins of these beliefs and experiences in traditional tribal world view and to trace continuities and discontinuities in these aspects of mentalité.

The documentation of mentalité may not always be congruent with the documentation of reality. In interpreting how people construe experience, anthropologist Clifford Geertz distinguishes between force and scope of cultural patterns. Geertz defines *force* as the intensity with which the pattern is internalized by people and its centrality in their lives, whereas *scope* is the range of context within which the pattern has relevance. Although scope in this sense is manifested by all three Dawn women in the application of their beliefs, the intensity with which they articulate these beliefs is more dramatic. What people have to work with in everyday life, argues Geertz, "is not the immediate perception of the really real, or what they take to be such, but the memory of such a perception."[46] Accordingly, this study of the mentalité of Anna, Patricia, and Tracie expresses their perceived reality as they remember it.

CHAPTER 2

HISTORICAL CONTEXT: WHO ARE THE CUPEÑO?

Honoring our ancestors: Mulu'Wetam
— *Motto of Cupa Cultural Center,*
Pala Indian Reservation

The Dawn narrations cast long shadows both forward and backward in time. To comprehend the present and the future of this urban Indian family, the reader needs to know about its past.[1] A tradition in the Dawn family is that of perpetuating a version of the names "Anna" and "May" through the generations.

Anna's grandmother, Anna May Smith Helm, whom everyone called "Gram," was Cupeño. She was born on July 9, 1885, in Escondido, California. During her teens she attended the Indian School in Carlisle, Pennsylvania. She married Steven "Box" Helm in a hotel, still standing, in Temecula, California, located in the heart of the traditional homeland of the Cupeño. Steve Helm was the son of Turner Helm, who had left his Missouri home with his five brothers and joined the migration west to California and the gold fields. Turner settled near Warner Springs and married a Cupeño, Mary Place. They had four children, one of whom was Steve, who

Anna May Smith, Anna's grandmother,
age nineteen

died in 1946 and was buried in the Indian cemetery on Pechanga Reservation.

During World War II, Anna May Helm worked as a riveter in a shipyard. Patricia was amazed when she heard that Gram had worked in the shipyards "in overalls." "I had always pictured her in the house, in the kitchen." Gram Helm died in 1973.

Belva May Helm, the daughter of Steve and Anna May, was born on July 4, 1907, in Mesa Grande, in a remote, quiet, and scenic section of traditional homelands high on a group of hills near Santa Ysabel. She attended school in Escondido and then, after the family moved to Los Angeles, completed her schooling in Compton. She married Charles King in the early 1920s but divorced him when her daughter, Anna, was about five years old and Anna's brother, Charles King, Jr., was about six. Although Anna knew very little about his family, she remained close to her father, an ironworker who died in 1988 at the age of eighty-eight.

Belva's many jobs included taking care of Bing Crosby's children and working as a baker, a receptionist for a doctor, a seamstress for the WPA Sewing Project, an inspector for a tire company, where her supervisors complained that she was too conscientious in her inspection responsibilities, and an assembly-line worker in a food cannery, where again she was criticized for rejecting less-than-perfect produce.

Anna May King, born on February 1, 1926, in Los Angeles, attended school at 103rd Street Elementary, Edison Junior High, and Jordan High School, all in south-central Los Angeles. She worked in a pickle factory and a distillery and held several waitressing positions, which she liked more than any of her other jobs. She married George Ryan in 1942. They divorced in 1946, and Anna married Harold Dean Dawn the same year. Patricia Ann, born on June 15, 1943, in Maywood, had a close, loving relationship with both George Ryan and Dean Dawn, calling them both "Dad."

George, born in 1924, had also attended school in Compton and was employed as a truck driver. The entire family grieved when he died in 1989. Born in Missouri in 1924, Dean attended school in that state before relocating in California, where he became employed as a truck driver and dispatcher at the same company where George worked. Dean and George became extremely good friends and remained so until Dean's death in 1988. Anna and Dean had one child, Steven, born on September 7, 1948, in Torrance.

Patricia Ann and her half brother, Steven, both attended Middleton Elementary School, Gage Junior High, and Huntington Park High School, all

Above:
Anna's mother, Belva, age ten

Below:
Belva, age eighteen

in Huntington Park. Pat has been almost continuously employed since graduation from high school. Her jobs have included work in a pharmacy, in a drive-in theater, and in numerous offices. Because of her variety of self-taught skills, she has been an office manager for a number of businesses, most recently for trucking companies. She married Tony Condello, the father of her daughter, Tracie. They were subsequently divorced, and Patricia had a brief marriage to James Nichols. Tracie has remained close to her father and his family, even after he relocated to San Jose, California.

Tracie Ann Condello, born on May 17, 1969, in Lynwood, had the same schooling as her mother, even having some of the same teachers. Tracie is currently attending Mt. San Antonio Junior College in Covina. Her employment has included sales and waitressing positions, and she continues to work part time while attending junior college.

The history of the Dawns is quite different from that of the majority of American Indians residing in Los Angeles. Most Indians migrated to the city under the auspices of the federally sponsored termination and relocation programs during the administration of President Dwight Eisenhower, when Dillon Meyer was commissioner of Indian Affairs. In a dramatic assessment of this urbanization, sociologist Howard Bahr has written, "The movement of the Indians to the cities, which began in the mid-twentieth century, may be as significant as the forced removal in the mid-nineteenth century."[2] Los Angeles was a major site for this urban relocation. Members of the Dawn family, however, had been living in Los Angeles for three decades before the massive relocation program. The urbanization of the Dawns was the consequence of significant

Above:
Charles King

Below:
Anna and her son, Steve, 1992

phenomena in California history: missionization, secularization, dislocation from traditional tribal lands, and conversion from a hunter-gatherer lifestyle to wage and subsistence labor.

The "Mission Period" of California history began with the establishment by Spanish Franciscans of Mission San Diego de Alcalá in 1769 and ended with the secularization of the missions by the Mexican government in 1833–34. The term *Mission Indians*, originally referred to all Indians who lived in the mission establishments or were under the care of the Franciscan fathers. The term continued to be applied to the descendants of those missionized Indians from San Diego to San Francisco, but in the classification of the Bureau of Indian Affairs, it was more narrowly applied to only those Indians living in the three southernmost counties of California: the Serrano, Cahuilla, Luiseño, and Diegeño (Kumeyaay) Indians.[3]

The term was also applied to groups, including the Cupeño, whose ancestors were never missionized but who lived near the missions in the desert and mountain areas east of the coastal strip. Florence Shipek, noted authority on California Indians, claims that many Indian groups hate the designation "Mission Indian" and insist on their band or tribal name.[4] In contrast, Anna recalls that her mother told her the family was Cupeño but also advised her: "Just say you're Mission Indian. That way then everybody won't foul it up. Just say you're a California Mission Indian" (12–31).

Despite the complex societies established by the indigeneous people long before contact with Europeans, the history of California has often been portrayed as beginning with the Franciscan missions, nine of which were established by Junípero Serra. Father Junípero Serra, a Majorcan Spaniard and Franciscan monk, earned a doctoral degree in theology at the age of twenty-nine. After serving as professor of theology at Lullian University of Palma, and later as a missionary in northern Mexico, he was sent with Gaspar de Portolá on the "Sacred Expedition" to take over the Baja California missions vacated by the expulsion of the Jesuits in 1767. The expedition was also intended to found new colonies in Alta California. In July 1769, Serra founded the first mission at San Diego.

The Franciscan missions were of a type known as *reducción*, or *congregación*. They were not built in an existing pueblo but were designed to gather (congregate) natives dispersed over the area, then "reduce" the Indians from their "undisciplined" way of life to Catholicism.[5] The missions were not solely religious institutions but were intended to bring about a total change in the culture of the native peoples in the shortest possible time. The padre would select an appropriate site, congregate natives of the area, baptize some of them, and then move on to a new site, leaving the actual construction of the mission to deputies, who relied on Indian labor in a feudal system. In this manner the chain of twenty-one missions, augmented by several *asistencias*, was established between 1769 and 1834.

California was a peripheral and frontier area of Spanish settlement, occupying a thin strip along the coast. Spain's colonization policies were a mixture of economic, military, political, and religious motives, with Indians regarded as subjects of the crown of Spain who were capable of receiving the sacraments of Christianity. Over fifty-four thousand neophytes were baptized during the mission period.

Efforts to sanctify Serra were begun during his own lifetime; more recently, in 1985, Pope John

Paul II declared Serra venerable, the first of three steps in the sanctification process. Serra's claim to sainthood rests on his work with the native peoples of California. Supporters have argued that the padre's humanitarian and saintly life was at all times exemplary, lifting the people under his care to a condition of well-being, physically as well as spiritually.

The campaign for Serra's canonization is, however, controversial. Whereas his advocates argue that the natives loved Serra and, without the Franciscans, were doomed to extinction, the opponents of Serra's sanctification argue that he was responsible for the conditions of slavery at the missions. Rather than rescuing the natives of California, the mission system, they contend, left a legacy of genocide.[6]

These conflicting arguments reflect the historic *La Leyenda Negra*, the Black Legend, and *La Leyenda Blanca*, the White Legend, associated with Father Serra's California mission system. The Black Legend, originated by the European rivals of Spain, was intended to discredit Spanish presence in the New World. Considerable propaganda described, in bloody detail, the Spanish mistreatment of the natives. This literature argued that Spanish claims should be invalidated and that more humane colonizers should take over, rescue the Indians, and properly develop the indigenous resources. The Spanish government, bolstered by accounts of friendly observers, countered with the White Legend, in which Spanish colonizers were depicted as especially humane, just, and enlightened.[7]

Intentional or not, the arrival of the Spanish missionaries unleashed destructive forces on the native population of California, profoundly disrupting the social, economic, and cultural structures of the indigenous peoples. Estimates of the precontact native population of California have ranged from

310,000 to 705,000.[8] Although analyses of the population decline of California Indians are vulnerable to the disparity of these figures, a decline as high as 90 percent has been asserted and attributed to the physical and social conflicts following contact.[9]

A number of scholars argue that the native peoples of California fared even worse under Mexican and American rule, although these scholars stress that this does not mean that the Spanish colonization was humane and enlightened.[10] Historical demographer Sherburne F. Cook attributes the difference between Spanish and American interactions with the native peoples of California to differences in modes of colonization.[11] The Spanish colonization was such that the invading and ruling caste was small in number. In California, the entire coast was taken and held by no more than one hundred men. Spanish missions were intended to be temporary. Thus, appropriation of native lands was not the issue that it became under Mexican and American rule. Spanish policy also envisioned retention of the natives as a population base. The Mexican and American colonizations, on the other hand, allowed no place for the native peoples. They were to be exterminated or segregated.

Early in the Spanish mission period, a small number of Cupeño entered Mission San Diego, but the majority were baptized after 1816 at San Luis Rey. During the entire mission period, unconverted Indians resided throughout the tribal lands of the Diegeño (Kumeyaay), Luiseño, Cahuilla, and Cupeño.[12] The Dawn family is representative of the Mission Indians who were even more severely disrupted by contact with the Mexicans and later with the Americans.

In early historical and ethnographic literature, the Cupeño were referred to as the Agua Caliente people, so named by the Spaniards because their village of Cupa (Kupa) was located near the mineral springs, now known as Warner Hot Springs, in northern San Diego County. However, scholar William E. Coffer notes: "Today it is virtually impossible to reconstruct these tribal units. They are gone forever."[13] Although very little of the tribal history has been retained by the Dawn family, Anna did recall the Cupeño being referred to as Agua Caliente (12–32). The term *Cupeño* is of Spanish derivation, an appending of *-eño* to the native place name of *Kupa* to designate a person who originates from Kupa.[14] Lowell J. Bean and Charles R. Smith, authorities on California Indians, state that the term *Cupeño* first appeared in the literature in 1906.[15] However, Charles F. Lummis, publisher and an advocate for Cupeño rights, used the term in a 1902 article. In "The Exiles of Cupa," published in Lummis's magazine *Out West*, he documented the Cupeño removal from their traditional homeland.[16]

Although relatively little literature exists on the Cupeño, among the smallest bands in California, scholars have found them to be a tribe with a rich culture and history.[17] At the time of contact in 1795, they occupied an area ten miles in diameter at the headwaters of the San Luis Rey River in what is now northern San Diego County.[18] Hunters and gatherers, they occupied two permanent villages, Cupa and Wilakalpa, which were at the junction of three major California groups: the Cahuilla, the Luiseño, and the Diegeño. Cupeño oral history regarding the mineral springs was recorded by P. L. Faye in 1921. The narrator, Salvadora Valenzuela, stated: "No one knows when the hot springs that were at our homes in Cupa were created. It is said the people arrived knowing about them. The water . . . came boiling up hot. And all the people said, 'It is our water.'"[19]

The Cupeño, like the Cahuilla and Luiseño, speak Cupan languages, a subgroup of the Uto-Aztecan family of American Indian languages. Cupeño oral history relates that the tribe originated as a branch of the mountain Cahuilla and that the tribe was formed eight hundred to one thousand years ago. The oral history is substantiated by evidence from research on their language and social organization.[20] An examination of the linguistic evidence led Alfred Kroeber to infer that one of two prehistorical events occurred: either (1) the Cupeño detached themselves from the Luiseño-Cahuilla group, moved out of the mountains into the San José de Valle, and were later "overtaken by their more numerous kinsmen," or (2) a small number of Cupeño moved into the valley and were later "crowded back into intimacy with [their] cogeners" by an expansion of the Hokan-speaking Diegeño, whose territory bordered that of the Cupeño on the east.[21]

The close and continuing relationship among the Cupeño, Cahuilla, and Luiseño has been noted by several scholars.[22] Intermarriage among these groups founded a new culture. According to Jane Hill, anthropologist specializing in Cupeño language and culture, this culture was "rooted in the Cahuilla tradition, but changed by an intricate interaction with the peoples around them. From the Cahuilla they derived a complex social organization, which included patrilineal clans, while from the Luiseño they acquired ethical and religious beliefs, including moral rigor, based on self-discipline, and the desireability of living an ethical life."[23]

Robert Heizer, noted authority on California Indians, believes that morality is an element of world view, but he finds that published ethnography is lacking information delineating the world views of native Californians.[24] There is no information in the *Handbook of North American Indians* in regard to Cupeño world view. Kroeber describes ceremonial rituals but nothing regarding world view or morality within the social structure of the tribe. William Strong, among other scholars, believes that although the Cupeño population was always heterogeneous, Cupeño have had the most intimate contact with the Cahuilla.[25] Anthropologists, therefore, have assumed that Cupeño morality, if delineated, would resemble that of the Cahuilla.[26]

In Cahuilla world view, the values stressed include tradition, respect for age, moderation and personal control, cordiality to in-laws, and reciprocity. Women are expected to be hard-working and to produce food efficiently, and a lazy person is considered a disgrace.[27]

What is known about the morality of the other close neighbors and kin of the Cupeño, the Luiseño, is derived from records of formal addresses to adolescents during puberty rites.[28] Values are remarkably similar to those of the Cahuilla. "What is enjoined," wrote Kroeber, "is purely ethical with reference to daily life: respect elders, give them food freely, refrain from anger, be cordial and polite to in-laws. Virtue is not only its own reward, it is the only path that leads to prosperity."[29] Accepting Hill's conclusion that the intimate and enduring relationship among the Cupeño, Cahuilla, and Luiseño forged a new culture group, I have relied on literature concerning all three bands in the discussions of ethical values, social organization, and the metaphysical realm. I refer to the Dawn women as Cupeño because that is how they refer to themselves. However, in this study, *Cupeño* signifies the group—identified by Hill—that has adopted aspects of Cahuilla and Luiseño cultures.

Bell tower at Mission San Antonio de Pala,
Pala Indian Reservation

The Cupeño had little interaction with whites for about a decade after their contact with the Spanish in 1795. By 1820, however, they had experienced dramatic changes in their life-style.[30] Where the Cupeño had freely hunted and gathered, Europeans now grazed cattle; the mineral springs at Cupa, which had become a health spa for the Spaniards, were now appropriated by the Mexicans and would later be usurped by the Americans; and several mission *asistencias* had been established on Cupeño land, notably San Antonio de Pala, founded in 1816 by Mission San Luís Rey, and Santa Ysabel, founded in 1818 by Mission San Diego. During this time, the Cupeño came under the influence of the Franciscans, and a chapel was built at Warner's Hot Springs. Although they became Christianized, the Cupeño maintained much of their traditional religion.[31]

The *asistencia* at Warner's Springs was abandoned after secularization of the missions. Secularization and the growth of the Mexican ranchos brought Mexican landowners into more direct contact with the Indians. The Cupeño, having learned agriculture from the Spanish, now worked for the Mexicans in serflike relationships, as they later would for the Americans.[32]

In 1844 Juan José Warner, a naturalized Mexican citizen originally from Connecticut, acquired title to San José de Valle, apparently by purchasing it from the former grantee, José Antonio Pico.[33] Warner's land grant, as Hill points out, "unfortunately did not mention the Indians" and referred to the lands as "vacant and abandoned."[34] Eyewitness accounts refute the inference that no Indians occupied the land. Lt. Col. W. H. Emory described the living conditions of the Indians at Warner's ranch in 1846: living in poverty, without adequate protection in temperatures dropping to thirty degrees, these Indians were held "in a kind of serfdom to the master of the Rancheria."[35]

In 1848, the Treaty of Guadalupe Hidalgo transferred California and the Southwest from Mexico to the United States. In 1849, the gold rush began, and miners joined the ranchers and farmers who coveted Indian lands. Indians in California began to experience the threatened destruction of their native economy as Anglos rapidly overran former native landholdings.[36] In 1883, Helen Hunt Jackson and Abbot Kinney, in their report to the commissioner of Indian Affairs, condemned white encroachment. "No one can visit their settlements, such as Agua Caliente, Soboba, Cahuilla Valley, Santa Ysabel, without having a sentiment of respect and profound sympathy for men who, friendless, poor, without protection from the law, have still continued to work, planting, fencing, irrigating, building houses on lands from which long experience has taught them that the white man can drive them off any day he chooses."[37]

In 1851, Antonio Garra, a chief of the Kavaly lineage of Cupeño, attempted to organize a revolt by southern California Indians against the oppression of Warner and other whites who had encroached on Indian land. Garra had established control over virtually all Cupeño groups, as well as other displaced native groups. The revolt was suppressed, Garra and his followers were executed, and the village of Cupa was burned.[38]

Southern California Indians gained some relief from encroachment between 1875 and 1877, when a series of executive orders created thirteen reservations—including Pala, a Luiseño reservation—for the Mission Indians.[39] The Cupeño continued to occupy the land around Warner's Springs, which Jackson and Kinney had described as "beautiful . . . well watered and wooded," with Agua Caliente clearly the most flourishing and influential of the five Indian villages in the area.[40]

Agua Caliente had formerly been set apart as a reservation, but the executive order was canceled in 1880. "The aged captain of the Agua Caliente Indians still preserves a paper giving a memorandum of the setting off of this reservation," Jackson and Kinney wrote. "He also treasures several other equally worthless papers—a certificate from a San Diego judge that the Indians are entitled to their lands; a memorandum of promise from General Stephen Watts Kearney, who assured them that in consideration of their friendliness and assistance to him they should retain their homes without molestation."[41]

Eventually the land became the property of John B. Downey, whose family sued in 1893 for the removal of the Indians. Although, with the assistance of Charles Lummis and the Sequoya League, the Cupeño fought the eviction, the Supreme Court of the United States decided on May 13, 1901, in favor of the Downey family.[42] After the decision by the court, Lummis argued in *Out West*, "These are not scalping savages who are being driven out of their immemorial home, but quiet, gentle, hardworking farmers."[43]

After the Sequoya League had failed to secure the traditional tribal lands, Lummis advised the Cupeño to decide where they would like to relocate. His mixed feelings about the relocation of the Cupeño are documented in *Out West*. "The Warner's Ranch Indians had in their old home a small and very poor territory. But it *was* their home, and they ought to have had it."[44] He also wrote that the Sequoya League "made every possible effort" on behalf of the Indians and, finding it impossible to secure the land, "did the next best thing, which was, in their judgment, to find a place so far superior to the dear old home that the next generation, at least, [would] be happier, safer, and better off."[45] In the search for suitable land for relocating the displaced Cupeño, the federally appointed Warner's Ranch Indian Commission, with Lummis as chair, inspected 250,000 acres of land, working 276 days of eighteen hours each. Finally, they decided on "a corner of Pala Valley," twenty-four miles east of Oceanside and twelve miles south of Temecula.[46]

Although Lummis claimed that Pala was far superior to the original Cupeño land, Hill states: "The Indians have never agreed with him. In fact they consider him a 'government man'!"[47] Yet C. E. Kelsey, in his report of 1906, described the Luiseño reservation at Pala as "undoubtedly the best in southern California." He wrote: "There is a large area of good land and a fine water supply. . . . The situation is certainly much better than that formerly occupied by the Indians at Warner's Ranch. It is not to be expected that the old people will ever be satisfied with any other place than Warner's Ranch, but the able-bodied young men are finding the value of the new location. They probably would not be willing to return to the old site, if it were possible."[48] Which of these accounts is the more accurate can perhaps best be determined by attention to the documentation of the removal of the Cupeño from Warner's Ranch; this information is found in the literature and also in exhibits at the Cupa Cultural Center, Pala Indian Reservation.

THE REMOVAL

Although the eviction of the Cupeño from Warner's Ranch is noted by a number of scholars, only one source, the articles in Charles Lummis's publication *Out West*, presents substantial documentation. According to Lummis, J. Downey Harvey, who controlled the collective interests in Warner's Ranch, declined to make any concessions to the Indians other than allowing them to remain on the land until a new location for them was acquired.[49] Lummis also wrote that except for the school, which was built by the government, everything at Agua Caliente was the work of the Indians, and that a conservative estimate of the value of the property was ten thousand dollars. He reported that 154 Indian residents were living at Agua Caliente. "I saw and talked with four generations in one family—all born here."[50] During talks with Lummis, one resident, Mrs. Cela Apapas, expressed the distress of the Cupeño:

You ask us to think what place we like next best to this place where we always live. You see that graveyard out there? There are our fathers and grandfathers. You see that Eaglenest mountain and that Rabbit-hole mountain? When God made them, He gave us this place. We have always been here. We do not care for any other place. It may be good, but it is not ours. We have always lived here. We would rather die here. Our fathers did. We cannot leave them. Our children [were] born here. How can we go away? . . . If you do not buy this place [for us] we will go into the mountains like quail and die there, the old people and the women and the children.[51]

Grant Wallace, of the *San Francisco Bulletin*, filed a story that was reprinted in the July 1903, issue of *Out West*. He reported that three of the "leading irreconcilables" spent nine days riding their "broncos" to San Bernardino "on a fruitless errand to beg President Theodore Roosevelt to 'intervene.'" While they were gone "chasing rainbows," a government Indian inspector, James E. Jenkins, arrived to supervise the eviction.[52]

Wallace wrote that night after night, sounds of wailing came from the adobe homes of the Indians. When Tuesday, May 12, came, many of them went to the little adobe chapel to pray and then gathered

Chapel at Los Coyotes Indian
Reservation (Warner's Springs)

for the last time among the unpainted wooden
crosses of their ancient burying ground. The pa-
thetic and forlorn group wailed out their grief over
the graves of their fathers. After loading "a little
food and a few valuables into their buckboard
wagons," twenty-five families drove away toward
Pala, followed by a wagon-train. The wagon-train,
trailed by a dozen of the younger Indians on horse-
back, "wound its dusty way over the mesa and
around the mountain roads."[53]

In 1962, Jane Hill recorded Rosinda Nolasquez's
memories of the removal:

First they said, "Go see your relatives for the last time
now." . . . They went to the cemetery, there they wept. Then it
was time to move out. Still they did not move. . . . They still
stayed there by the gate. And my great-grandmother went
running into the mountains. And she said, "Here I will stay,
even if I die, even if the coyotes eat me." . . . The people
moved out from the cemetery. They were weeping. And
then from there they moved us. . . . And they said to them,
"Now, look behind you, see your homes for the last time."

But no one turned around. . . . They did not look back again. They were very angry. And they said, "Tomorrow up there some time that water will dry up, and then you'll learn your lesson."[54]

Nolasquez remembers that when "they threw us out," the Cupeño lost all their belongings. "We went away and left, the chickens were left behind. We lost everything."[55] She recalls that when they arrived at Pala, "There were no houses, so they dumped us outside."[56]

Wallace, who had accompanied the Cupeño on the journey, reported that on arrival at Pala, the Indians' "bitterest complaint" arose from what they perceived as the impossibility of keeping their clothing and bodies clean. "At Agua Caliente it had been a matter of pride with them to keep their linen spotless, and each person took a bath in the hot springs every day." Wallace found that at the end of his two-week stay with the Cupeño, "many of the older people were still '*muy triste*.'" Although "devout church members," the Indians refused the first Sunday to attend services in the Pala mission, asking the visiting priest, "What kind of a god is this you ask us to worship, who deserts us when we need him most?" Instead of attending church services, they conducted a *sooish amokat*, a rabbit hunt. Observing that the Indians would have at Pala a village similar to their old pueblo at Agua Caliente and also the advantage of "aloofness from elbowing whites," Wallace concluded, "There would seem to be no reason why these Indians should not soon be happier and more self-reliant at Pala than at Warner's Ranch."[57]

Four years later, Special Agent C. E. Kelsey reported to the commissioner of Indian Affairs that this particular band of Indians had been making

Saint Anthony, patron saint of the
Mission at Pala

adobe and living in adobe houses for more than a
hundred years.[58] The idea of constructing the emi-
nently suitable adobe houses at Pala was rejected
by the government, however, because it would take
too much time. Since the Indians were inclined to
be mutinous, threatening to return to Warner's ranch,
fifty portable houses were ordered by the government from New York. It was nearly six months
before the Indians got into the houses, and the
expense was four times the cost of adobe houses.
"The houses are neither dust-proof nor water-proof,
and are far inferior to the [rejected] adobes."[59]
Today, driving through the Pala Indian Reservation,
one sees weathered and worn wood-frame dwell-

ings. The only adobe structures are in the Mission San Antonio de Pala compound.

Because the removal from Warner's Springs to Pala occurred in May, this month has assumed great significance for the Cupeño, especially those living on the reservation. An annual observance of the removal is held at Pala on the first weekend in May. On May 4, 1974, the Cupa Cultural Center was dedicated at Pala. Prominently displayed in the center today is a mural of ceramic tile. Created in 1981 by Clifford Antonio "Tanty" Diaz, the director of the Cupa Cultural Center, the mural depicts the Cupeño "Trail of Tears" during their removal from Warner's Springs. An adjacent photo display documents the Cupeño saying goodbye to the graves of their fathers at Warner's Springs, loading their buckboards for departure, and then moving into the "temporary" portable houses at Pala. One photo captures images of sacred stones, with initiation ceremony marks, which were left behind at Warner's ranch. Another is the last photo taken of "old Manuela," who took to the mountains rather than relocate and was never found.

The accounts in *Out West* of the grief of the Cupeño at being forced to leave their ancestral land, substantiated by the exhibits installed at the Cupa Cultural Center more than seventy years later, indicate that even Lummis underestimated the Cupeño's passionate attachment to place. The priests of Mission San Antonio on the Pala Indian Reservation have observed in the Indians of the parish a strong attachment to place. The Indians tend to go back to Warner's Springs, often wanting to be buried there. Sister Mary Yarger, the former principal of the Mission San Antonio de Pala School, observed that attachment to place also extends to Pala. She noted people who have left and later return, but

Legend of the Mission San Antonio de Pala

even more significant, people who never want to leave.[60]

In the Dawn family, there appears to be a marked change over time in attachment to place. The memory of the removal from Warner's Springs has faded, although there is a handwritten note, author unknown, among the family papers that reads: "Cupeño Indians evicted from village of Cupa (Warner Hot Springs) in May, 1903, and moved to Pala Mission, founded June 13, 1816." "It was a shame," says Anna. "It really was a shame. It could have been handed down . . . 'cause, you know, those mineral baths . . . I imagine they charge a fortune to go in there" (3–33).

Anna recalls that when her grandfather, Steve Helm, became homesick for the traditional Cupeño areas around Warner's Springs, he would "get in a little old car and he'd take off." Occasionally, the women would decide to meet him there. Sometimes they would "see his car and he'd have it open with his feet hanging out alongside the road . . . [near] Lake Elsinore or up in the mountains" (3–27). Other times, "He wasn't there when [the women] got there," and they would make inquiries throughout the rural communities. "Have you seen Helm?" (3–27). "They all knew my grandfather, I tell you. Around Julian and Pala and everywhere. They all knew my grandfather" (2–7). The responses, therefore, were personal and friendly: "Oh, you mean 'Box'? Yeah, he's down the road." The women would find him, "sure enough . . . just sittin' there, looking. Alone. Just sitting there, you know" (2–7). Helm insisted that he be buried on the Pechanga Indian Reservation, near Pala. The family does not know why Steve Helm selected Pechanga. Since Pechanga is Luiseño, it is not clear if he was able to prove Luiseño blood or if Pechanga Reservation, like Pala, accommodated Cupeño. But Steve "Box" Helm was granted his wish.

Anna's mother, Belva May Helm King, evidently felt a strong pull from the areas around Pala. Anna remembers: "My mother liked the quietness out there in Pala and Julian and all those places. . . . She loved the quietness [but] she also loved to go to the pow-wows" (12–41). Anna has not visited these areas as frequently as her mother and grandparents did, but she too feels a pull and regrets that she cannot go there more often. Although she recalls hating to go there as a child, she says: "Now that I'm older, I want to go there more. I guess because my mother loved this area so much. That's all she talked about. I love to go there now too and just walk around the area."[61]

Like her mother, Pat remembers that she did not like visiting the reservation when she was younger because "it's out in the middle of nowhere" (4–1). Like her grandmother, she values quietness, but "anywhere it's quiet" is attractive to her. She enjoyed a weekend she spent in a cabin in Twenty-nine Palms, where there were "no phones, no TV, no radio." She read and slept the entire weekend because it was so quiet. "You could hear a car five miles away. And like you could reach up and grab the stars" (18–14). With no memories of her rare visits there as a small child, Tracie is even more removed from attachment to the areas around Pala. She has not, however, developed an attachment to Huntington Park. She says she would like to live somewhere else. She is not sure where, but it would be out of Huntington Park (11–19).

Sister Yarger has observed that it is very difficult for people to leave the Pala area, but they do so for higher education and to improve their employment potential (23–9). When asked where the young people go when they leave the Pala area, the sisters agree with other residents of Pala that the urban centers of San Diego and Los Angeles are the most attractive (23–10).

This type of rural-urban migration is the continuation of a pattern that began in the mid-nineteenth century. As early as the 1860s, native workers who could not find steady employment near their homes often traveled to Los Angeles, where vineyards, stockyards, and a busy commercial district offered employment. Laborers from the Indian settlement around Temecula worked in Los Angeles but returned home for fiestas and other special occasions.[62]

Unlike certain other aspects of native culture that were rapidly eroded under the impact of acculturative influences, fiestas continued to be important contexts for both social and religious interaction.[63]

In their narrations regarding the attractions that lure them to the reservation areas, both Anna and Pat use the term *fiesta* more often than *powwow*. Hill, in her dictionary of Cupeño, lists *fyeesta*, borrowed from the Spanish *fiesta*.[64] In the museum of the Santa Ysabel mission near Temecula is an unpublished manuscript written by Marian and Stanley Davis, early settlers of the area. They describe the Indian celebration of the Fiesta de las Cruces of 1903: "The Santa Ysabel natives are hosts and their friends will come from tribes scattered far and wide, from Mesa Grande, Warner's, San Felipe, Campo, Cahuilla, and from the fields and factories where some of their members have wandered from the reservations to seek employment from the white man. It will be homecoming for them."[65]

The federal census of 1860 reveals that Mission Indians had already mastered a variety of occupations in addition to those related to agriculture, including vaquero, servant, cook, whaler, laborer, shepherd, miner, and woodchopper.[66]

Anna vividly describes the work of her grandmother, Anna May Lawson Helm, on a white-owned ranch near Mesa Grande: "I think she cooked for about twenty-five to thirty men . . . every morning the same thing, hot biscuits and gravy and ham and bacon and fried potatoes and eggs. Every single morning." (1–35) "It made her feel so good knowing that they liked her cooking. . . . [But] she didn't go into baking apple pies and things . . . [because of] doing all the housework and everything." (1–37) "She had two big wash tubs out in the yard, and she had to carry that water and heat it, [carry] the wood, and everything. So she was a real work horse" (1–38).

After 1900, Indians who had previously derived their subsistence from the ranches near the reservations began to move to cities.[67] Although migration patterns of American Indians are sometimes difficult to determine accurately because of disparities in methods of identifying Indians in census reports, scholars have detected a continuing strong movement toward Los Angeles.[68] Mission Indians, who had been working on white-owned ranches like serfs, joined the migration to Los Angeles.[69] The Dawn family exemplifies this urbanization.

URBANIZATION

The direction of migration, uniformly toward the centers of white population, resulted in the formation of an Indian urban class.[70] In 1910, there were 831 California Indians living in towns, three times as many as in the period between 1890 and 1900. Rapid urbanization continued in response to the demand for urban labor during both world wars and to the availability of the automobile for transportation.[71]

The 1980 census reported that nationally, 63.8 percent of the 1,420,400 American Indians lived in towns and cities. California has the largest American Indian population, over 200,000, with 50 percent of these living in the Los Angeles and Long Beach urban areas. Although many urban historians perceive a close relationship between ethnicity and race in the cities, this relationship is elusive in regard to American Indians. Howard Bahr suggests that American Indians are "invisible" in the city.[72] He attributes this invisibility to four factors: (1) an extremely mobile population, moving from the city to the reservation; (2) low visibility of Indians, who often "pass" as whites; (3) functions of support handled by the Bureau of Indian

Affairs; and (4) non-Indians' belief that *urban Indian* is a contradiction in terms that creates a dissonance in a cherished stereotype. Are these four factors pertinent to the Dawn family?

The interviews clearly indicate that the Dawns, rather than being mobile, are extremely stable in residency. Five generations of this family have lived in essentially the same area south of central Los Angeles since relocating to the city around 1920. As to visibility, although Anna physically appears more Indian than the others, all three women usually are assumed to be white. She talks about people's surprise when, knowing that Anna is Indian, they meet Pat and Tracie. "They never had occasion to meet any Indians like that. . . . They were surprised when they seen Tracie's hair, her blue eyes. And my daughter's. . . . [On] my mother's side, just one uncle and myself and my grandfather . . . had blue eyes or blue-green. The rest of them had big black eyes" (3–53).

Although Anna's mother was perceived as being something other than white, she was usually not immediately identified as Indian. Anna tells a story about her mother, who had been patronizing neighborhood bars for years during the 1940s and was suddenly being refused service.[73] "Somebody had gotten mad at her, and she thinks it's one of her girl friends." The friend informed the bartender that he was serving an Indian. "And the guy says, 'What do you mean I'm serving an Indian? There are no Indians in here.'" The troublemaking friend responded that there was an Indian who came into the bar all the time. When informed it was May Helm King, he could not believe it. "May? May's an Indian?" He confronted May: "You know we cannot serve Indians in here. At all." Anna's mother retorted: "Well, I'll just go down to another bar, if you won't serve me." May's friend, however, went ahead of her "to all of these little bars and [told] them that they were serving Indians and they could get in trouble" (1–11, 12). Anna recalls that they would not even serve her a Seven-Up in the bar (1–14) because she was May's daughter (1–13).

A similar incident occurred when Anna lost a job in a distillery because someone told the management that she was Indian; her boss decided she could not legally work in a whiskey-bottling plant. Yet when asked if they were Indian, no one in the family thought to lie (1–17, 18).

Although the Dawns typify the low-visibility factor referred to by Bahr, his assertion that functions of support for urban Indians are performed by the Bureau of Indian Affairs (BIA) appears to have little relevance to this family. However, Pat would like Tracie to be registered with the BIA "to show that she's part Indian, and it's part of her heritage" (13–1). When Anna, Pat, and Tracie were asked to whom they would turn if in need of help, no agency, government or private, was mentioned. Without exception, all three would turn to immediate family for support (18–25, 28, 19–1, 21–1, 2).

Pat colorfully articulates her encounters with Bahr's fourth factor, the idea that urban Indians violate "a cherished stereotype." She recalls what her stepchildren thought: "I had walked off of the reservation and had feathers in my hair and the whole thing." They believed that they would live with their stepmother in a tepee. "You know, they didn't know what a tepee was" (4–21). Moreover, she resents some remarks from fellow employees. One said: "I hear you had a war party last night. You were out drinking firewater" (4–50).

Despite the factors that Bahr saw as perpetuating the low visibility of urban Indians, in 1972 he predicted that the invisibility of the urban Indian could be coming to an end because of increased political activities, "Red Power" movements, and pan-Indianism.[74] However, in a 1986 *Los Angeles Times* article "The Plight of Native Americans on the 'Urban Reservation,'" Tom Sellars, a northern Montana Blackfeet who had lived in Los Angeles for twenty-five years, stated: "We are faced with various socioeconomic problems, but the largest and most perplexing problem is our inherent lack of visibility. We are an unseen and unheard voice."[75] In October 1989, the *Times* reported on Indians in Los Angeles in an article entitled "The Invisible Minority." Lincoln Billedeaux, chairman of the Los Angeles County American Indian Council on Aging, a private advocacy group, said: "We are an invisible minority in Los Angeles County. We have no geographical neighborhood, such as Koreatown, or little Tokyo, or East Los Angeles. People think we are from some other groups, because we come in all colors."[76]

Anna agrees that Indians are the invisible minority and attributes this phenomenon to a lack of individual leaders and to Indians' reluctance to assert themselves (9–45). Pat concurs with her mother's assessment. "[Indians] are basically quiet people. They don't want to make problems. I guess they're afraid that if they start something, something [bad] will happen, and that they should basically stay in the background and let somebody else take all the credit for what they've done or haven't done" (13–22, 23). Perhaps because of her own experience, Tracie believes that some visibility can be achieved by being registered with the Bureau of Indian Affairs. "For people to . . . show, prove that they are Indians, . . . that they're registered. . . . If they have kids, they should be

registered, . . . so they can be part Indian too"
(11–47).

They may be less visible, but research suggests
that for Indians, as for other minorities, the most
important factor in Indian migration to urban areas
may be economic opportunity.[77] Although there
were probably other factors affecting the decision,
Anna believes her family was motivated to move to
Los Angeles because, as previously noted, there
were job opportunities. Evidently her mother was
especially adept at developing a variety of employment skills. Working as a housekeeper for a doctor,
she was able to substitute for his office employee
and eventually worked her way into full-time employment in the office (19–18).

Urbanization does not, however, necessarily improve economic conditions for American Indians.[78]
In 1987, a comparative study of ethnic groups in
Los Angeles found that 20.5 percent of American
Indian women and 16.8 percent of American Indian
men in the city of Los Angeles were living below the
poverty line.[79] When asked what she remembers
about the financial situation of the family when she
was growing up, Anna responds, "It was very poor."
She remembers that they "never even had money
for medication" (19–17). Her grandmother "made
biscuits and gravy" if they had nothing else to eat
(7–30). "A lotta times," recalls Anna, "she didn't
have the flour. So we didn't eat. You know, we didn't
get anything. No biscuits or anything" (7–33).

Despite an apparently comfortable economic situation now, Anna painfully remembers that in the
1920s the family went to government-sponsored
food depots, "where they would have a truck dump
off a sack of potatoes and whatever there was. . . .
Potatoes or turnips." She adds: "That's why I can't
eat a turnip to this day. . . . And sometimes we would

get down there, [and] there would be so many people that had to eat and had big families [that] we'd get there and there wouldn't be nothing." She remembers that as a child of six or seven, during these trips to the food depot, she would pray that "there would be something left" for her family (7–30, 31).

Later, married with her own small children, Anna sometimes "didn't know where the next meal was coming from." She says: "I didn't have any potatoes, no nothing. Oh, God what are we going to do?" Her husband, Dean Dawn, who had recently been hired by a trucking company, had not yet received a paycheck. Near where they lived was a small mom-and-pop grocery. Her husband declared: "You know something? With all my pride, I'm gonna go down and ask them if I can get some credit until I get paid" (19–31). That evening, he came home with groceries. "The guy let him have some groceries. I was so, I was so thrilled, I couldn't wait to get into the sacks to see what he bought" (19–31).

The economic plight of urban Indians is seen by many scholars as virtually overwhelming and the root of all their social problems. With American Indians joining other economically marginal people in the cities, some scholars conclude that rural-to-urban migration may not be the best solution.[80]

Alcoholism is one of the problems that is perceived by some scholars as having roots in the economic deprivation of Indians.[81] Kathryn Grandstaff, director of the Indian Mental Health Clinic in Los Angeles, reports, "At least 80% of our clients have substance abuse problems." But Grandstaff maintains that alcohol and drugs are not the etiology of their illnesses. "Major depression and identity crisis are the causes of alcoholism, not the reverse."[82]

Both Anna and Pat remember Indian men becoming belligerent when drinking. "At the fiestas," Anna says, "they drank, . . . and one guy'd look at another cross-eyed, and that starts the whole thing. And they would get into pretty good fist fights" (1–38). Pat recalls: "I've seen Indian men drink. And they get very nasty. Fighting would break out" (2–60). When asked if any of her family members behaved in this manner when they drank, Anna responds: "No, they'd just . . . get more or less argumentative, you know, but not in fist fights. They'd just holler and stuff like that" (1–39). Anna's memory of her grandfather "getting thrown out of a lotta bars" near Pala (2–7) does not coincide with Tracie's belief that he never touched a drink in his life. The disparity may be due to the fact that Steve "Box" Helm died before Tracie was born, or it may be due to the desire on Tracie's part to refute the "drunken Indian" stereotype.

Another problem associated with economic marginality is substandard housing.[83] However, Indians, residing in all types of housing, are scattered throughout the Los Angeles area, with small population bulges in Cudahy, Bell Gardens, Huntington Park, and parts of Long Beach, El Monte, and Maywood.[84] When asked if her family had experienced discrimination in urban housing, Anna relates that her grandmother, hoping to rent a house in the Watts area of Los Angeles, was confronted by the landlord with inquiries about her race. "I'd like to know a little bit more about your race and where you were born," explained the landlord, "because people tear up the places, you know." Anna May Lawson Helm retorted, "We ain't pretty, but we are never tearing nothing up" (9–5).

A review of the literature on urban Indians may seem to corroborate the depressing argument of German sociologist Georg Simmel in the late nineteenth century that urban residency leads to alienation and deviancy. Anthropologist Ronald Cohen, however, declares: "If alienation is a malfunction of modern society, ethnicity is an antidote. . . . Ethnicity provides a fundamental and multifaceted link to a category of others that very little else can do in modern society."[85] Moreover, I believe that Simmel's theory had the major flaw of omitting the family as shock absorbers. Anthropologist Joan Wiebel has concluded that humans make rational decisions about their lives, that migrants to the city attempt to retain the values and behaviors that sustain quality of life, whether these values and behaviors originated in the city or in a rural community, and that the family as a social and economic resource is a salient and continuing factor.[86] Jeanne Guillemin, in writing about urban Micmacs in Boston, specifically credits the family for sustaining quality of life. "Urban Indians develop their cultural strategies in an area beyond the comprehension of the wider society, namely in the domain of family and tribal organization."[87]

Despite these and other scholars' recognition of the importance of Indian family life, surprisingly little research has been done on the Indian family in an urban setting.[88] One of the rare studies involving urban California Indian families is a three-year field study of 120 families residing in Oakland and environs. Although the dates of the study, conducted by the Native American Research Group, are not specified in the final report, the data indicates that it probably was undertaken in the early 1970s. Of the 120 urban Indian families interviewed, 30 were Sioux, 30 were Navajo, 30 were from "selected tribes," and 30 were from a variety of California tribes, the names of which are not specified.

Noteworthy comparisons between the California Indians and the other tribes emerged in the Oakland study. Whereas high percentages of all tribes reported seeing their relatives often, 100 percent of the California Indians claimed to do so. In response to the question of who gives assistance in emergencies, California Indians tied with the Navajo, with 86 percent reporting that they first ask for assistance from relatives, as do the Dawns. California Indians reported the highest number of households, 20 percent, that included extended family members. Another similarity to the Dawns is the finding that at 8 percent, the California Indians in the Oakland study were the least able of the tribes to use their tribal language, as compared with 40 percent of the Sioux and 30 percent of the Navajo.

However, some statements regarding ethnic pride by interviewees in the Oakland study are in stark contrast to the expressions of Anna, Patricia, and Tracie. "Many California Indians grew up afraid and ashamed of being Indian," one interviewee claimed. "[They] would take Mexican names or try to marry into Mexican families due to the white prejudice toward Indians." The report states, "Over and over, California Indians told us that they came to the city to get 'lost.'"[89] Despite such statements, the Oakland study concludes, "The sharing of life with extended family is an important cultural residual."[90] The centrality of the family is dramatic in the narrations of the Dawn women. Cultural change or persistence is consistently revealed through the prisms of family relationships in the mentalité of Anna, Patricia, and Tracie.

CHAPTER 3

PERCEPTIONS OF FAMILY AND INDIVIDUALITY

I am related everywhere.

> —*Cahuilla expression
> of pride, privilege, and power*

The Cupa Cultural Center on the Pala Indian Reservation displays memorials for deceased persons in the form of ceramic tiles, created by the director of the center, Antonio "Tanty" Diaz. The tiles are inscribed with not only the names of the children and grandchildren of the deceased but also the names of grandparents, great-grandparents, and great-great-grandparents. One tile reads: "In loving memory of our beloved mother, grandmother, great-grandmother, great-great-grandmother, aunt, and great-aunt. We love and miss you dearly."[1] How does a family maintain so much integrity over so many generations?

Although the family has been recognized as the mainstay of the continuation and endurance of American Indian culture, Robert Ryan found, in a review of the literature on the American Indian family, that most of the scholarship focused on negative aspects. "It is time," he argues, "to begin the process of identifying strengths that can be passed on to future generations."[2] Sister Mary Yarger is passionate about this phenomenon of focusing on negatives. "We have to stop this, this sense of failure. . . . That is a personal goal of mine. . . . If we look at failure, we'll fail. We have to find the positiveness. . . . Otherwise, we're wasting our lives. We're just absolutely wasting our lives, and I refuse to do that" (23–13).

A method for identifying strengths in American Indian families is suggested by asking, "How is the family equilibrium developed and maintained?"[3] If we apply this question to the Dawn family, Anna, Patricia, and Tracie, all three, declare that no one outside the family has exerted influence on them. Pat says: "I have friends. I have good friends. But not to the point where they would be an influence on me. I've worked for every ethnic group there is. . . . They were good people. . . . But I can't say anybody from outside the family has ever [been] an influence, you know. Other than my family" (4–28). She sums it up: "The Indian family is very close. Very tight. Very together" (4–28).[4]

Anna expresses an identical sentiment. "Patricia and I, we're very, very close. It's the same way with my mother and my grandmother both. We all got along. We helped each other, and if they needed help, we'd be the first ones there. Like I said a hundred times before, we could talk about our own family, but we didn't want anybody else saying anything about 'em. 'Cause that would start a doings, you know. We were, are even yet, a very affectionate family" (17–43). Pat, in separate interviews, echoes her mother's sentiment exactly. "Don't talk about my family. No outsider better ever say anything [negative] about my family" (14–23).

Anna believes that having kids of her own drew her closer to her mother and grandmother. "[My mother] helped me an awful lot. . . . She was always right there. And always willing to do something, if I was busy with the kids, you know. She'd go in and start dinner or try to mop or do the washing or something like that. . . . I'll tell you, her and my grandmother they were so beautiful. It's just hard to believe. Everybody that met them said that they just couldn't believe it. I mean, the closeness of the family" (17–49). The pride, the sense that family closeness is a virtue, is echoed by the comments of one of the priests at the Mission San Antonio de Pala church. When asked what the majority of the community at Pala would consider a virtuous man or woman, he responded without hesitation, "Someone close to the family."[5]

How is this closeness generated and maintained? The answer is suggested by another group of tiles in the Pala Cultural Center, these inscribed with the names of "Honored Members" of the center. When asked how they became honored members, "Tanty" Diaz responded, "They are the elders."[6] This commitment to the elders is embodied in the motto of the Cupa Cultural Center. "We honor our ancestors: *Mulu'Wetam*."

THE ELDERS

As in Cahuilla and Luiseño tradition, in Cupeño tradition age was a criterion for privilege, power, and honor. Deference to elderly people was protected by tradition, which allowed the elders to function as repositories of knowledge and lore. The life history of the Dawn family is imbued with deference, but also with affection, for the older generations.

Anna remembers that it would "just thrill" her mother's father, Steve Helm, if his granddaughter

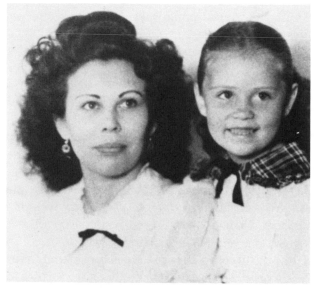
Anna and Patricia, around 1949

did something special for him. "I'd make tapioca pudding from scratch, and say, 'That's for you.' Nobody else could eat it. You know, anything he asked, I would do it for him" (3–6). It was Steve Helm who gave Patricia her Indian name, "Little Tobet," meaning Little Rabbit (2–10). Pat's narrations are full of fond memories of her maternal grandparents. Of her grandfather, she says: "We were close. . . . He'd hardly ever say anything, but he'd sit and grin. Or he'd walk up and pat me on the shoulder [and say,] 'Whatcha doin,' honey?'" Her grandparents had Frank Sinatra albums that she loved, so she would sit with her grandfather and play phonograph records for hours at a time (4–22).

Although the patrilineal emphasis in precontact Cupeño, Cahuilla, and Luiseño societies has been noted by a number of ethnologists, patrilineality does not mean that the societies are patrifocal, and the pattern of the Dawn family reflects a pronounced emphasis on the women. Despite Pat's fond memories of her grandfather, an inquiry about who had the greatest influence on her when she was growing up elicited this response: "I think my mother and my grandmother. My great-grandmother" (13–53). With affection and appreciation, she says that she still sometimes will lie back and think about her grandmother's efforts to visit Pat's newborn baby so that Tracie would know her great-grandmother.

Pat also remembers staying with Anna after giving birth to Tracie. "I'd wake up and my mom would be at the bassinet picking her up, so she wouldn't wake me" (13–53). She recalls being "scared to death" of her newborn baby. "She was so little. My mom, my grandmother, and my great-grandmother, they showed me what to do and how to do it" (18–25).

There has been no discernible change over time in regard to respect and love for elders in the Dawn family. Tracie, after the divorce of her mother and father, came to regard her grandparents as surrogate parents, since Pat found it necessary to work full time. Pat compliments her parents on this role. "They raised [Tracie]. They brought her up really great, I think" (13–50). Despite a strong attachment to her step-grandfather, Dean Dawn, who raised her, Tracie also maintained close ties with her biological grandfather, George Ryan. "My grandpa Dean was like a father to me. My grandpa George was like my grandpa" (11–29). However, in response to an inquiry about people who influenced her, her statement is nearly identical to that of her mother. "The people that I'm really close to is my grandmother. And my mom. . . . That's who I sit down and talk with. Just them" (8–7). About her daily visits with Anna, she says, "It's always been like this." When she awakens in the morning, she first goes to Anna's house for a cup of coffee and to "stick around and

Tracie, age six

talk." After school or work, she visits Anna, then again in the evening. "I'm always bugging her. I love her, that's why" (21–9).

A mother passes on not only the messages of her culture but also the messages she received from her mother. Thus interactions between a mother and a daughter may be interactions among three generations.[7] In speaking of her children, Anna states, "I tried to raise them the way I grew up: respect your elders" (17–51). Tracie articulates the persistence of this mentalité in the Dawn family. "I respect my elders. If my grandma needs something, I'll go out of my way to get it for her" (8–13).

Sister Yarger expressed a refreshing and realistic attitude toward the elders of Pala: "If the elders respect themselves, o.k. You cannot be an elder and be nasty to everyone else and expect everybody to love you. . . . I think we're aware of the elders, but it's a twofold thing" (23–8). This concept of reciprocity is a pervasive value in tribal culture[8] and is reflected in Tracie's mentalité. Expecting to help her older relatives, she knows she can also depend on them. When asked to whom she would go if she needed help, Tracie responds with confidence, "I could go to my mom." But she adds: "My grandma mostly. . . . My grandma, she understands everything." She perceives her grandmother as understanding her "a lot more" than her mother does. "I guess 'cause she's been around a lot longer" (21–2). Although the three women form a tightly bonded group, there does appear to have been some change in mother-daughter dynamics during the last generation. This change is revealed in their individual narrations, which are remarkably consistent with each other.

NEYE WIW: CUPAN FOR MY MOTHER AND ME

Anna had a mother-daughter dream during the time of the interviews. She was riding in the car with her grandmother, her mother, and Pat. Her mother was also Pat's mother, and Anna complained, "You pay more attention to Patricia than you do to me." Her mother responded: "No, I don't. I love you both the same." Even her grandmother scolded Anna: "Your mother loves you both the same. Stop squabbling."[9] This dream, having perhaps an emotional logic, reveals the intensity of the relationship between Anna and her mother, an intensity also demonstrated in the narrations. Moreover, it suggests the family's view of people who attempt to assert ego and individuality: everyone is loved identically, and questioning this elicits disapproval.

Anna and Pat perceive their own relationship as having ideal unity. "Sometimes, we'll more or less think alike. . . . Both of us say the same thing at the same time, and we have to laugh at each other." Or

Anna will say only, "Do you remember?" And Pat, intuitively knowing what her mother is remembering, will articulate Anna's thoughts (17–34, 35). Pat describes this congruence of thinking between herself and her mother. "We know what the other person's going to do before [she does]." She observes that she and her mother work extraordinarily well together because they think and feel alike (18–15, 16). When asked if she and Tracie work this well together, an apparent change in mentalité emerges. Pat laughs and responds: "Oh, Lord. No, no. She's good [but] she has a mind of her own" (18–16).

In the literature on mother-daughter relations, these relationships are discussed in the framework of the achievement of independence. Intergenerational closeness is perceived as a source of distress for each generation.[10] How can one explain that a lack of separateness may cause distress in some families yet result in feelings of considerable pride and satisfaction in others, like the Dawns? Is there potential for alienation in families like the Dawns? Three aspects of mentalité—discipline, anger, and privacy—have proven to be useful avenues in exploring these questions with the Dawn family. How are these aspects perceived? Are these perceptions perhaps related to tribal values?

Because Anna's mother, Belva May Helm King, worked outside the home to support her family, Anna and her brother were left in the care of Anna's grandmother, Anna May Lawson Helm. In this respect, the urban family was following the tribal tradition of the older women caring for children and teaching them the knowledge necessary for adulthood while the younger women were busy collecting and processing foods.[11] Anna vividly remembers her grandmother's discipline. "I wanted to stay after school, but I always had to come home and do my work, then set the table and help her cook. . . . I told her, there's a game on, or something, and I wanted to stay [at school]. She told me no. And, well, I stayed. When I got to the house, she didn't say anything. She just got up from the table and whacked me. And I mean that little woman was strong" (1–49, 50).[12]

Belva May Helm also had been raised by Anna May Lawson Helm to believe that "when you were told to do something, you didn't ask why, how come. You did it." Anna articulates her mother's resultant style of child rearing. "When she told you to go stand on that mountain, you [would] go stand on that mountain. You wouldn't ask why or how come" (1–46).[13]

Sometimes when she had misbehaved, Anna thought her mother would forget, but she notes, "My mother never forgot" (1–47). "She was like an elephant" (17–50). Anna also remembers that her mother had "quite a temper." "She wasn't a cruel mother, . . . but what hurt worst [was that] she'd make us go pick our own switches. . . . That was really terrifying, you know. And I always tried to find the skinniest one I could. That didn't work either. God!" (17–50).

Both her mother and her grandmother insisted on decorum at the table. "You go there for one purpose, that's to eat." But Anna remembers that she and her brother would be "kicking each other underneath the table," and they would get sent to bed without anything to eat. "But it was real cute. My grandma came in with some food and gave it to us. . . . Here come my mother through the other door [bringing] food to us. So we had a ball" (1–48). The behavior that angered her mother the most was Anna's "bickering" with her brother. "That's one thing my mother always said: 'There's just the two of you. You take care of one another'" (1–47, 48). If they disregarded this warning, they were invariably switched.

As an adult, Anna approves of the way in which she was raised. When asked to compare her childhood discipline with the way she raised her own children, Anna responded: "Just about the same. I try to . . . get it as close [as possible] to the way I was raised." When she told her children to do something, and they responded: "Do I have to?" or "Well, I will in a minute," she notes: "That was a no-no, with me. . . . The way my mother [raised me] and her mother taught her, . . . I try to raise mine more or less the way I was raised" (19–6, 7). A story that Anna tells about Patricia's white oxford shoes dramatically illustrates a persistence in her attitude toward disciplining children.

Anna had purchased white oxfords for Patricia. "And it was so funny. She hated those things. . . . I said, 'You're going to wear those shoes.' You know what that little devil was doing? She'd go out the door, hide them in the bushes, take her good shoes and wear those, and before she come in the house, she'd change shoes." Anna happened to see the white oxfords where they were hidden in the bushes. "I left them right where they were. She come in and I said, 'How do you like your shoes now?' [Pat answered,] 'Oh, Mom, they're great!' And I says, 'Patricia, don't lie to me. . . . I saw those oxfords in the bushes. What have you been wearing to school?' Well, she was wearing her good dress shoes. To school. I said, 'O.K., for that when those wear out, you don't get any more dress shoes. You're gonna have one pair of shoes only.' Her dad thought it was funny. I mean, he just thought that was really funny. He says, 'Boy, that kid outsmarted you'" (17–23, 24). Anna, however, administered a "triple punishment" to Pat. "I wouldn't let her go anywhere for a week. Her girlfriends couldn't come over here, and Pat couldn't go anywhere. And she couldn't use the phone. She hates 'em [oxfords] to this day. She does" (17–25).

As an adult, Pat apparently still feels some constraints on her behavior. When asked if she is ever "rowdy," she replies: "I don't like to worry about everybody . . . watching or condemning me. . . . You know, certain people saying 'Don't do that, or that's not nice, or stop that, or you've had enough.'" When asked if anyone has made these remarks to her, she laughs and responds: "Yes. My mother" (18–4).

There appears to be some change occurring with Patricia in regard to discipline. "I had my own Madonna. . . . She's a rock singer," narrates Pat. "I came home one night, and I looked at her [Tracie], and her hair was standing up like this and out like this. So I took her in the bathroom and I combed it out. Came home the next night and it [Tracie's hair] was back up there again. But she [Madonna] was her idol, so she patterned after her." When questioned as to how she handled this attempt by Tracie to assert a separate self, Pat responded: "She outgrew it. I wanted to see how long it would continue. And I guess she got tired of it, and so she stopped it. . . . I ignored it" (18–17, 18). Tracie's account is identical to her mother's. She says that conflict with her mother arose mostly because of Tracie's hair and makeup. When asked how the conflict was resolved, she responded, "I just started growing up, I guess" (21–8).

Despite this apparent change on Pat's part, she articulates the pattern established by her mother, grandmother, and great-grandmother. "Well, I like discipline. . . . You don't do this. You don't do that.

I'm very strict with her [Tracie]. She's gonna be twenty in May [1989] and she still has a curfew" (13–50). Tracie sustains this view. She approves of the curfew and tells her friends: "My family does worry about me. And I'll be the same way with my kids" (21–18).

Another avenue for exploring perceptions of individuality is the manner in which anger is expressed. When asked if the women in the family were the disciplinarians or if her grandfather also disciplined her, Anna responds: "He wouldn't talk to me. That's how he hurt me" (1–50). She relates the following incident, which occurred when she was about fifteen years old. Her grandfather and his Indian friends were having a big party.

It was the early timers, with violins and banjos and all that stuff, . . . the old time dances, you know, how you swing your partner. . . . Well, I didn't know how to do that kinda stuff. [My grandfather] said, "Come on, Granddaughter, dance with me." All I said was, "Oh Pop, I don't know how to do that stuff." He didn't say one word. The next day I got up to cook his breakfast. I was talking to him [but] he didn't answer me. I said: "What's the matter, Pop? Don't you feel good?" And you think he'd answer me? . . . Just because I told him I didn't want to dance, I didn't know how to do that, . . . he wouldn't talk to me for one solid month. . . . He wouldn't eat what I fixed. . . . Finally, I made this great big bowl of bread pudding. . . . He didn't touch it. . . . I tried: "What did I do?" He wouldn't answer me. He was stubborn. And I mean stubborn. I couldn't figure out what the heck I'd done. . . . If I

Opposite Page Above:
Patricia, age thirty

Opposite Page Below:
Tracie, age eighteen

would come into the room, he'd get up and leave. . . . [After a month] I said, "Pop, I'll do anything for you. Don't be mad at me. It's hurting me. I don't know what I done." He was working underneath the car, and then he came out and he says, "Well, you did embarrass me. My own granddaughter didn't want to dance with me. That hurt. To think that you wouldn't dance with me. . . . It's o.k., I'll never, I'll never ask you again to dance." And, by God, he didn't. (I–50–53)

The conflict was fueled by Anna's refusal to dance with her grandfather. Since contact, observers have recorded the importance of dancing to Mission Indians.[14] The desire to be able to perform Indian dances is repeated throughout the interviews. Steve Helm's manner of showing his displeasure with Anna is also intriguing in light of both tribal and family history. Formal advice during tribal puberty rites stressed that people must refrain from openly expressing anger.[15]

Expressing anger with silence has been a pattern in the family. Anna describes her adult relationship with her mother. She says, "It's unbelievable, but we did get along beautifully together, and we enjoyed doing things together" (2–2). But she also admits that they would occasionally have "little spats." She says: "See, when I get mad, I get quiet. And it would kill her, when I wouldn't answer her. And the only way she could, what she would do is run back there [to the house in the rear] and make some pies. Or cakes. And then she'd stand at the door here and knock on it. . . . She'd knock. 'May I come in?' I said: 'I don't care.' [My mother would ask,] 'Well, do you want me to or not?' And she'd stand there holdin' these pies, you know, or cakes. . . . That was her way. She wouldn't say she was sorry, though. And I was ornery. I wouldn't say I was sorry. Bein' stubborn. Well, like I said, we did get along beautifully together" (2–2).

Pat remembers objecting to visiting the reservation. She remembers, "My grandmother made me." If Pat refused to go, her grandmother "used to get upset and would not talk." Pat says, "Like my mother, you know, like my mother." When asked how long her mother or grandmother would refuse to talk to her, she responded: "I guess until I did something, you know, . . . little things for my grandmother, trying to get back on her good side. 'Grandma, can I do this [for you]? Grandma, can I take you for a ride?' [Or I would] bring her home a little something from where I worked" (2–23, 24). Why would her grandmother become angry? "Because I would believe in my rights. . . . Like my hair. . . . [My grandmother would say,] 'Don't cut your hair,' What'd I do? I'd go out and cut my hair! But, see, we were very close to her" (2–24).

Apparently, there has been a change in mentalité with Patricia in the expression of anger. "Me, I'm the opposite. I get mad, and my mouth starts running. I don't care. . . . I say what's on my mind and that's it. I explode, and then get over it. My mom is very quiet. My grandmother was quiet, and I'm just the opposite. I'm very mouthy" (2–23). Anna disapproves of Pat's way of expressing anger. "When she blows a gasket, I say, 'You're gonna fall over with a heart attack, if you don't calm down. Do something, go watch television or something'" (15–39).

Evidently, Pat's way of expressing anger is a model for Tracie. "She has a temper. She has a temper," Pat says of her daughter. "She rants and raves and stomps and storms." Such behavior is not permitted by Pat, however. "She'll walk by me and I'll grab her hair and I'll yank her down. She calms down. She sits there, and I keep looking at her, and then she'll start grinning, and then she'll start laughing" (18–6, 7).

In addition to attitudes toward child rearing and toward expressing anger, a third avenue exists for investigating mentalité regarding family and individuality: the concept of privacy. Patricia remembers that when she was a child, the family always went places together. "We never went separately. . . . We always went as a group" (2–46). Today, since she works full time and spends Saturdays with her mother, Pat is adamant about reserving Sunday for herself. "Sundays I kinda stay to myself. That's my only day that I have to rest. . . . My mom knows that's the only day I have, and she's real good about it. . . . [Tracie also] is real quiet, because, like I said, Sunday's the only day I have" (18–15).

Anna feels that she herself has the right amount of private time. "Sometimes I just want to be here by myself" (17–30). She expresses the dynamic by which she and Pat have worked out their individual needs. "We check on each other. . . . We find out what we're gonna do for dinner. . . . We trot back and forth to see what each other's doing" (17–45). When asked if she perceives any disadvantages in this arrangement, Anna replies: "Well, in a way, like if I'm trying to get dressed, and I think they're back there, and the next thing you know, they're in here. . . . My children have never seen me running around nude in front of them. I say: 'Don't you people knock? Don't come in when I'm dressing.'" Pat teases her, "Oh, Mother, you're not that shy an Indian." Anna retorts: "I am, too. I'm bashful, you know." Anna concludes this "complaint" with the affectionate comment, "We kid each other" (17–46).

Tracie talks with obvious pleasure about the times she spends with her mother as well as her grandmother. "My mom likes to go [to amusement parks] so I take her [or] she takes me. . . . We just have a good time together." When asked if she ever does anything by herself, she laughs. "All alone? No." She does think that "everybody needs to have a little private time alone." When she feels this need, she would like to go for a long drive, but since she doesn't have a car, she stays in her room and reads (21–4). She would like to listen to music, but "different people have different tastes in music." When asked which people don't appreciate her taste in music, she admits: "My mom. My grandma" (21–5). In response to an inquiry as to whether she perceives any disadvantages to being in such a closely knit family, she replies: "No. I think it's great. I really do." She observes that some of her friends envy her family. "They call my mother 'Mom' and my grandmother 'Grandma'" (21–15).

Patricia relates the most dramatic manifestation of the family's view of individuality and private time. At the age of eighteen, she had her own apartment. "They [her family] weren't too thrilled about it. But, you know, I was on my own. I was working. Well, they were always there, when I came home. They wanted to surprise me; they'd bring groceries or something Grandma baked. You know, they'd come by and see what I was doing. My grandmother would come over, and my landlady got to know her, and she would let her in" (20–3).

Despite a remarkable congruence in mentalité through several generations, Pat expresses ambivalence regarding family and individuality. "Our family was very, very close. That's very bad. Because, let's say, if I was to get married again, and my husband wanted my affections all to himself, . . . I couldn't hack it. Because I am too closely involved with my family. My family comes, I guess, first. . . . And a lot of people don't understand that. They don't understand the closeness we have" (2–25).

Rivalry for affection evidently is perceived by Anna as an indication of closeness. She appears rather proud of the fact that her husband "was a little jealous of me, and I was a little jealous of him" (15–50). In regard to jealousy of people who have more material wealth, however, she says: "Oh, no, no, no. I'm never jealous of what anybody else has got, . . . or how they got it. More power to them. . . . I've never been envious of anybody that has, you know, things" (15–51). For Anna, belonging is far more important than belongings.

Despite her mother's tolerance for jealousy in personal relationships, Pat clearly perceives a potential for alienation in this type of conduct. She blames both her divorces on jealousy. Tony Condello "used to slam the door in my mother's and my grandmother's face, when they came over to visit. He was ornery [and] would make my mother and grandmother seethe. . . . He'd come out of the bath, [see Anna and Belva May, and then say,] 'You here again?'" (18–20). Sometimes Pat was not home when Condello insulted her family. "But when I found out about it, I'd chew him. We got into it" (18–21). Condello evidently claimed he was joking, but Pat countered, "You don't do that with my family" (18–22).[16] Although her second husband, James Nichols, got along well with Pat's family, she nevertheless describes him as "a very jealous and possessive man" (4–24).

Despite the potential for alienation, when asked directly whose needs should come first, the family's or the individual's, the Dawn women indicate a persistence in mentalité. Anna says: "I think the family should always come first, because it keeps them together. I think the family's [needs] should come first" (15–33). Tracie replicates the sentiment: "The family. Because you have more people to support than just yourself" (11–42). A priest at the Pala mission suggests that the rural tribal view is much the same as that of the urban Cupeño. "The first choice is the family, but for them, also, the tribe is a family" (22–10).

AMERICAN INDIAN FAMILY STRUCTURE

There is very little in the literature regarding the Mission Indian family per se. It is apparent, however, that "when other aspects of the society broke down or changed, the extended family persisted."[17] Similar to the Dawns, the Cahuilla extended their kinship system beyond the nuclear family to embrace five generations.[18] It must be noted, however, that Joan Weibel-Orlando concluded from her study of elderly Indians in Los Angeles that the large, multigenerational Indian family household is a stereotype. She qualifies this finding slightly: "Even though many older people may not be living in close proximity to their families in Los Angeles, that doesn't mean they don't keep in contact. It does mean it is much more difficult to keep up traditional and expected family ties in this urban setting."[19]

Throughout the five urban generations, the Dawns have maintained households that were more extended than nuclear. These households have blended varying combinations of the families of Anna's great-grandmother, Louise Lawson, born around 1860; Anna's grandmother, Anna May Lawson Smith Helm, born in 1885; Anna's mother, Belva May Helm King Jewett, born in 1907; Anna May King Dawn, born in 1926; Anna's daughter, Patricia Ryan, born in 1943; and Anna's granddaughter, Tracie Ann Condello, born in 1969.

During Anna's second marriage, to Dean Dawn, the blending of her household with that of her mother, Belva, appears to have been particularly successful. In traditional society, an ideal spouse fulfilled his kin obligations: respecting elders, getting along with in-laws, and being a good provider.[20] Although Dean Dawn was not a California Indian, he evidently was an "ideal" husband. In response to an inquiry as to how Dean felt about the extended household, she says: "[Belva] claimed him. Everyone thought he was really her son, . . . 'cause she always called him 'son.' She never said, 'This is my son-in-law, [but] this is my son, [and] I don't want anybody to say anything bad about him.' He called her 'mom', and they'd do things for each other. She'd bake him all kinds of pies. . . . He never resented her once. If we got low, she'd help us out financially. And if she needed anything, we'd do the same for her, you know" (17–40, 41). Although she was not in close contact with her first husband, George Ryan, for a while after their divorce, Anna says, "It just seemed like we were meant to get together, . . . and share the family, the families, you know" (18–37). Anna's narration of how the families got together is one of the most colorful vignettes of the life history of the Dawns.

Well, this is funny. This is real funny. My husband [Dean] drove a truck for Safeway. . . . And George also drove a truck [for Safeway]. Well, unbeknownst, they got to talking one day in a restaurant. Dean says: "Why don't we meet over lunch, and I'll buy you a cup of coffee and a piece of pie?" So they took turns. This went on for a long time. He come home and he says: "I met this George. . . . He wants us to doubledate . . . for a nice dinner sometime. . . . He just asked me if I was married, and he said he was married." I didn't think anything of it. So, anyway, they decided to come over here. And when he

[George] walked in, and he looked at me, and I looked at him, I just about passed out. I couldn't believe those two knew each other for years, having coffee together, you know.

And she [George's wife, Betty] was standing there, looking at me. It just struck me funny, and I said: "There can't be two of you. There just can't be two of you." [George] said: "Well, what about me? When [Dean] said 'Anna,' it didn't dawn on me." And we got to laughing. Well, we did go [to dinner]. We got to laughing so hard. And we just started talking. 'Course it was something, sitting there with ex's and everything. [Afterwards] we got together [again] and we went out to dinner, and we have been doing that ever since. We laughed and we laughed, . . . and ever since then, we've been the best of friends. (18–39–41)

Although Pat feels she was closer to the dad who raised her, Dean Dawn, than to George Ryan, she loves them both very much. She is very happy about the blending of the families. "When Betty and Mom and I get together, it's just like three kids. We have a ball" (18–34). "Everyone thinks I am her [Betty's] daughter. We have a good relationship, . . . which makes it good for Tracie. . . . I don't have to separate for the holidays. . . . We all get together and we all have a good time" (18–30, 33). She notes her fondest memory: "When I got married, both [fathers] walked me down the aisle" (18–29). "I couldn't hurt either one of them. I wanted them both there, you know" (18–33). She recalls that the minister who performed the ceremony used Pat and her two fathers as the basis for his sermon the following Sunday. "He said he had never seen anything like this in the many years that he's been in the ministry. He said it's something very unusual to have a family that close" (18–36).

Anna and Patricia express amusement over the confusion created when members of Dean's family

Tracie and her step-grandmother, Betty,1991

and of George's family were introduced to people who did not know the family structure. Pat says, "My one girlfriend, she's gotta have a scorecard, you know [to keep the relationships straight]." Anna remembers that the family from both sides would "all come over to one place or another for dinners, and we'd all pitch in and get there early and try to help." But when she was introduced as George's ex-wife, she says, "You know right away that it don't ring a bell" (18–37). While kinship terminology in English is inadequate for such sophisticated relationships, Pat resolved the confusion somewhat by referring to Dean and George as "Dad One" and "Dad Two." Otherwise when she said "Dad," both men would respond. "I go: 'Not you, the other one'" (18–35). She characterizes the relationship between her two dads, "They were like brothers." Dean Dawn died in February 1988. "And my dad, he says he lost his brother when my dad died" (18–33).[21]

Divorce did not destroy the interrelationships of the Dawn family. Pat maintains close contacts with the families of both her ex-husbands. Of James Nichols's parents, she says: "His family and I are very close, to this day. I am their daughter. . . . [They call me their] number one daughter" (4–17, 18). When she and Nichols divorced, she wanted to keep his children. "But he wouldn't let me have them." The children have remained close, however. They call Pat "Mom" and Anna "Grandma" (4–19). Tracie says of Nichols's daughter: "I'm still close to my sister today. My step-sister. I call her my sister" (8–34). Tracie also refers to Condello's children, who are about fifteen years younger than she, as sister and brother. "I love 'em. I'm really close to my sister. She might be my half-sister, but I'm still close with her" (8–34). To Tracie, the term *step* in connection with relatives is irrelevant. "It doesn't matter if they're 'step' or if they weren't born into the family, I'm going to be close to them. Because that's how I am with my family. I love them, and I want to be loved back" (11–29).

The concept of reciprocity is strong in Tracie's expectations. When she felt she was not receiving the kind of love from her father that she was giving him and his family, she phoned Tony Condello. "It was the first time I ever yelled at my father. . . . I told him: 'You don't treat me like a daughter. I don't feel like you love me. I'm tired of crying for you. . . . I'm not going to cry anymore.' It hurt. . . . He knew he hurt me, because he's been acting a lot better now" (8–33).[22]

Anna narrates a story that indicates not only a persistence of expectations of reciprocity but also a persistence in the belief that significant nonkin are considered family. When Anna's husband Dean Dawn and her father, Charles King, both were terminally ill with cancer, the family decided to care for them at home. Anna was near exhaustion from the work and sorrow. "One of my friends did offer to come and help me with my husband and dad. . . . We were real close. . . . She said: 'You was good to my mother and my daddy.' And I said, 'Well, I loved your parents, you know. . . . I wanted your parents to be included with my family.'" The friend insisted, "I'll come and help you, because you're going to crack up if you don't get help."

After she had been in Anna's home a short time, Charles questioned Anna regarding the arrangements for paying the friend, and Anna replied: "Well, Dad, . . . we didn't even talk about it, you know. And she didn't say anything about paying. . . . I've bought her clothes and everything and took her out to dinner. Maybe that's not enough. Now, she's supposed to be my friend, and I'd do the same for her. For her family."

Anna's father, wanting to thank the friend, gave her a check. "She just grabbed it." Anna was shocked. "You'da thought she never had seen a check, you know. . . . I was saying to myself: 'Don't take it. I mean, show me that you're my true, true friend, [that] you did this out of the kindness of your heart.'" When her friend took the money, Anna was thinking: "That's it. I'm through with her. . . . She preferred money to my friendship. That did hurt me, that money came before a friendship" (15–21–24).

Anna's narration dramatizes scholars' arguments that in marked contrast to the nuclear family structure, which stresses independence of its members, American Indian family structures assume mutual responsibility through interdependence.[23] A priest at Pala has observed that a member of the Pala community "must not go simply [toward] an individual goal. There must be a sense of community"

(22–2). Nowhere else in the Dawn life history is this perception of community more evident than in their feelings and their behavior when family members are ill.

Anna remembers that the entire family helped with her terminally ill husband and father. Pat and her brother, Steve, and Tracie would come home from work and immediately help Anna. "Lotta times they didn't get to eat dinner til ten, eleven o'clock, because [of] trying to get them both cleaned up and rubbed down and fed" (15–38).

Pat explains their decision to care for Dean and Charles at home. "We care. We have feelings, I guess. A lotta families don't have feelings, because I know families that have stuck their mothers in a home. . . . I could never do that. . . . I just can't do it. I could never stick my family in a home. We had my great-grandmother [Anna May Lawson] living down the street when she was ninety-some years old. [After a stroke] we brought her out of it. My grandmother [Belva May Helm] brought her out of it, working with her night and day, . . . and she had the family to help her. [Anna May] improved slowly but surely. She got on her feet" (13–54). Anna Dawn recalls the family's group effort: "My poor mother didn't get much rest, . . . that's why we tried to go out and help 'baby sit' my grandmother, while my mother went out for a while" (15–46).

Tracie believes that she learned valuable lessons taking care of her grandfather and great-grand-father. "I learned that no matter how sick a person is, you don't send them to a home [and] let somebody else take care of them. They won't get well unless you take care of them" (8–22). When she talks about her devotion to Dean Dawn, her sense of reciprocity is dramatic. "I loved him very much. . . . He was always there for me, when I needed him.

Whenever I needed anything, he'd go out of his way to get it. Or to teach me" (10–6).[24]

Sister Yarger refers to Indian families as having a "fragile stability," which can be easily disrupted. However, she adds that "if there is someone there to care and to take care," the disruption will "heal better and quicker" (23–3, 4). Are there, however, disadvantages inherent in this type of family structure? Some observers may perceive these potentially negative consequences in the Dawn life-style. Family members, by their own testimony, do not have the benefit of diverse influences; individuality is suppressed if it presents a threat to the family; constraints on behavior may persist into adulthood; there is a potential for alienation, especially for individuals who marry into the family; and privacy may be sacrificed for togetherness.

Are these disadvantages balanced by strengths in the family structure? The family that is, as Patricia describes, "very close, very tight, very together," provides an unfailing source of support. Statements like "Don't talk about my family" are rooted in a shared mentalité. Moreover, this support most often is manifested in what Sister Yarger termed "someone there to care." This caring is especially remarkable during times of stress, such as childbirth or illness. The participation of the elders in the vital happenings of the family provides flexibility in child care and consistency in preserving family values. Although discipline is a salient factor in the Dawn family, it appears to be tempered with love, as exemplified by Anna's mother and grandmother, who brought food to the children who were sent to bed without supper.

Although there is potential for alienation, there is also potential for in-laws to be embraced and supported as though they had been born into the family. In the Dawn family, terms like *son*, *daughter*, and *sister* are flexibly and generously applied. Despite prevalent concern about what Sister Yarger calls the "fragile stability" of contemporary Indian families, death and divorce have not destroyed the integrity of the Dawn family structure. The lack of privacy is a problem only if it is perceived to be by the family members. Although Anna mildly complains, she appears to have an affectionate tolerance for her daughter and granddaughter's habit of continually coming in and out of her house. She knows that they "bug" her, as Tracie puts it, because they love her.

Will the commitment to the famly persist in the mentalité of future generations of Dawns? An indication that it may is evident in Tracie's response when asked if she will raise her children as her mother and grandmother raised her. She says, "I'm going to have them help me raise them" (21–18).

CHAPTER 4

BENEFICENCE

Mamayu: *Cupan for "to help"*

Anna tells a story about a time when she was moved to help someone. While at the meat counter in a supermarket, she overheard an elderly couple. One spouse said to the other, "Well, Honey, we'll have to wait and get it next time." Anna told them to select the meat they wanted, and she would pay for it.

They thought it was some kinda gag or I was on TV or something.... They'd say: "Well, o.k., what do you want? What are you selling?" And I said: "I'm not selling anything."... And they said: "Are you serious?" And I said: "Yes, I am.... Please, you pick out what you want." I said: "Please. We will go together to the [checkout] counter."... So we went up there; the little people went ahead of me.... And I told them to wait right there at the end of the counter. And they still didn't understand what I was trying to do to them.... But, see, I felt that they didn't have the money to buy the meat. (5–4, 5)

The checker was a friend, and when she realized that Anna was purchasing the meat for the couple, she exclaimed: "Anna! What are you doing?" But Anna recalls, "[The couple] thanked, and they thanked, and they thanked me" (5–4, 5).

Anna remembers telling her late husband, Dean Dawn, what she had done. He said: "You know something, honey? I did the same thing the other day. When I went to the store, there was this little old lady. . . . I wanted to put my arms around her because she reminded me of my grandmother." Dean reported that the elderly woman picked up several packages of meat, putting each one down, shaking her head. With a generosity identical to Anna's, he purchased meat for the woman. "She thanked, and she thanked, and she kept saying, 'God bless you.'" Dean told Anna, "I did it because I felt I needed to do it." Anna concludes this story, "That's the way we were" (5–6).

One could easily conclude from these incidents that Anna and her husband were moved to help elderly people. The reality is that their sympathy was not limited to this group, as dramatized by another narration.

[Two] little kids in a hamburger place . . . wanted one hamburger, and they were going to split it. Well, I'm standing there, and I felt like a nut, because I'd ordered cheeseburgers and french fries and cokes, and I'd listened to these little kids say, "Well, we can split it. But we don't have enough for french fries and cokes." So I just listened a bit [until] they asked the [counter employee]: "Could you please cut it in half?" That's when . . . I said: "Are you kids hungry? . . . Would you like two burgers? And french fries? . . . What would you kids like to drink?" And those kids stood there lookin' at me. . . . They asked if they could [help carry] my stuff home, they were so thrilled." (5–9)

A short while later the kids were telling some friends: "See that lady up there with that man? . . . She bought us the food." When asked what she would have done if their friends had asked to be treated to hamburgers also, Anna responds that her husband offered to buy food for the friends. When these two boys politely refused, Dean Dawn insisted.

Anna's beneficence is mirrored in the narrations of her daughter. Patricia has her own stories of helping people in the supermarket. "I feel sorry for them," says Pat, "because somebody is elderly, and they have to stand there and count their change to buy a quart of milk. I say: 'Just put it on my bill.' I feel good that I'm helping somebody. . . . I do it because I want to do it. [But] they can't believe it. Somebody my age helping somebody their age." To a question regarding whether it is always the elderly that she helps, Pat responds: "I've helped . . . young kids that didn't have enough money. . . . Little kids will come in [to the market] and they'll want something. You know they want it real bad. And I say: 'Go ahead . . . I'll take care of it.' And a lotta times the manager will thank me. . . . You see 'em standing there counting their pennies. And I figure, God, I hope somebody does that for my daughter" (13–2, 3).

Although Indian families are not unique in being beneficent, Pat's relationship with her parents has influenced her perspective on beneficence; moreover, these personal relationships within the family have effected a similar morality in Tracie's view of life. When asked, if she had a ten-year-old daughter and someone came to the door needing money, what she would say to her daughter, she responds: "I'd give 'em some [money]. . . . And if [my daughter] goes: 'Well, why did you give them money?' I'd tell her because they need food and maybe they don't have no groceries in the house and no clothes . . . for the kids. I'd try to make her understand" (10–18).

How do we interpret these stories of generosity? James Clifford, writing about "partial truths," states, "There is no whole picture that can be 'filled in,' since the perception and filling of a gap lead to the awareness of other gaps."[1] Expressing a similar perspective, Clifford Geertz has written, "Understanding the form and pressure of . . . natives' inner lives is more like . . . reading a poem than it is like achieving communion."[2] Nowhere is this elusive quality of interpreting mentalité more apparent than in the Dawn narratives of beneficence.

In her study of assistance patterns of American Indians in Los Angeles, Joan C. Weibel concludes, "Humans make changes and shifts in coping strategies when former behaviors are no longer viable, . . . but tend to maintain those which work and are valued."[3] Why, then, is beneficence an enduring and valued behavior for the Dawns in an urban milieu? Can this behavior be attributed to a persistence of Cupeño values? Is it related to the concept of reciprocity or to concern for the elderly? Is this beneficence a manifestation of ethnic cohesiveness? Are kinship and friendship networks involved? Is beneficence an identification with the poor? Is adherence to earlier teachings a factor? Is the behavior perhaps unique to the Dawn family? Exploring these questions does not provide definitive answers but does suggest several possible interpretations for the enduring and genuine generosity of the Dawns.

TRADITIONAL VALUES

Two related aspects of morality that recur throughout the ethnographic literature on native Californians are the belief in the interrelatedness of man and nature and the belief in the value of reciprocity. "Native Californians," wrote historian Jack D. Forbes, "perceived themselves as being deeply bound together with other people."[4] This concept of inter-relatedness is congruent with the fact that reciprocity has been a pervasive value in the view of native Californians. Paul Kroskrity, professor of anthropology at UCLA, states, "Native Californians are well-known for extending kinship to neighboring groups, for positively valuing cultural borrowing, and for engaging in reciprocity and exchange."[5]

Can the narrations of the Dawn family be interpreted within the framework of interrelatedness and reciprocity?[6] Of the jobs Anna has had, the one she liked best was working in Clifton's Cafeteria in Huntington Park. "People would come down the line, and I'd look at them, . . . and someone would look so pitiful, and they'd look so hungry, so I'd always give them more than I was supposed to. And that's why I liked it" (1–40). Although she tried to make the portions look smaller so as to avoid detection by the manager, she was approached by him. "I know what you're doing," he told her. "I was watching you" (1–41). He asked her if she had been giving extra-large portions for quite a while. "I said: 'Yes, I have.' I didn't lie to him." He directed her to give everyone standard portions. She remembers:

Every once in a while I'd slip a little bit more on or find the biggest piece of meat I could. . . . You can judge people just by looking at them. You really can. And I knew they didn't have any money. Especially a lotta these elderly women would come in, little tiny things, you know. And it would just about break my heart. They'd just pick out a certain thing they could buy a la carte. Like they'd get a dish of macaroni and cheese or [something] that is filling, but they didn't have no vegetables or anything. And a lotta times, . . . I bought the food and put it on their table. I still do that. If I see somebody in a restaurant, . . . and they don't have [enough] money, I still do that. (1–42, 43)

BENEFICENCE
95

Although there appears to be a sense of inter-relatedness, there is no direct reciprocity involved in this narration. Like other stories related by Anna and Pat, this one reveals concern for the elderly, but the extension of this concern to other age groups is dramatized in the following narration. Anna and Dean, while driving to Las Vegas one day, stopped at a coffee shop en route.

It was windy [and cold], . . . and this poor young guy, all he had on was a thin, short-sleeved shirt. . . . He didn't dare to sit in the restaurant without ordering. . . . He walked up to my husband and said: "Sir, I'm so cold, . . . can you afford enough for a cup of coffee?" . . . My husband, . . . he said: "I'll tell you what. You go to the counter, and you have the waitress give us the check." Well, all he got was a doughnut and a cup of coffee. And the waitress come over and she says: "You mean to tell me you're gonna pay for his food?" . . . And [Dean] said: "You tell him to get a steak dinner." So she went back and told him, and he didn't know what to do. I mean, it embarrassed him. . . . He got a hamburger, . . . and he kept drinking coffee. He was shaking so bad he could barely hold that cup of coffee. We got up to leave, . . . and my husband gave him [an extra] ten dollars. . . . I thought he was going to cry. I thought he was going to get on his knees. He said the other ones just ignored him when he asked for a cup of coffee. That's all he wanted, to get warm. . . . So he followed us outside and he said: "God bless you." He said: "God bless you." (I–45, 46)

Although there is little probability of repayment by the young man in this story, Anna hints at a belief in a universal reciprocity. When asked where she learned about this kind of beneficence, she responds: "Oh, from my folks. I mean, my parents. They always believed, . . . and that's the way it usually turns out, when you give, you usually receive.

Like my mother, she always gave her last dime, . . . if somebody was hungry or something, then just within a few days, she'd get money from something, you know, in return" (5–3). Patricia also indicates an awareness of reciprocity when she tells of helping children in the market and then says, "God, I hope somebody does that for my daughter."

Although the original values of reciprocity and interrelatedness appear to be essentially intact for the Dawns, these values may have undergone changes in the city. To identify these changes in the Dawns' mentalité regarding beneficence, it is useful to explore four factors: ethnic cohesiveness, kinship and friendship, perceptions of class, and adherence to earlier teachings.

ETHNIC COHESIVENESS

Patricia indicates in her narrations a persistent identity with Indians. A considerable sacrifice of her valuable time was involved in work at the Indian Free Clinic in Huntington Park. As a single mother who worked full time during the day, she volunteered at the clinic five nights a week for three years. "I'd get off work, come home, see my daughter, then go down there [to the clinic] and work until about nine. Come home and get ready for bed and do the same thing all over again [the following day]" (2–55). Her mother and grandmother took care of Tracie during the evening because "they thought it was great" that Pat was helping at the Indian clinic (2–56). "I enjoyed it," says Pat, "because I was working with my people." When asked if she would have worked for an Irish clinic, since she is half-Irish, she answered: "No. . . . There's a lot of Irish people around. And there's very few Indian people" (4–26).

Despite her efforts to assist non-Indians in need, Anna tells a story about one occasion when she chose to help Indians rather than whites. She and Dean were driving through the reservation areas near Hemet when Anna noticed an Indian family selling strawberries from a flatbed truck alongside the road. "They were dressed so horrible. I felt so sorry for them." Because of traffic conditions, Dean could not stop and suggested they "catch the next one" selling strawberries. The next family selling berries alongside the road was white, however. "And selling their strawberries a few cents lower than what the Indians had." But Anna was remembering the Indian family. "That truck was so dilapidated. Honest, to God, it made me sick. And the kids didn't have no shoes on. And the little dresses, you know. No sweater, no nothing." She wanted to "turn around and go back to the Indians," but Dean insisted on continuing because they were on the way to Anna's father's house. "Your dad's gonna be real upset if you're late." Presently they encountered another Indian family with a flatbed truck. "They had old torn Levis on. I mean, the knees were all out and everything. That just about broke my heart. I said to my husband: 'Pull over.'" When Anna and Dean got out of the car, the man asked them what tribe they belonged to. He told Dean that he recognized that Anna was an Indian. "I can spot an Indian a mile away. Those cheekbones and that nose, that straight nose." When they asked how much the strawberries were, he replied, "Well, for my Indian friend [a bargain]." Although the weather was hot and the berries had to be transported in the trunk of the car, Anna insisted on buying two lugs of berries. Dean protested, "They're gonna be rotten before we get to your dad's." But he good-naturedly purchased the berries. While her husband was putting the lugs into the trunk, Anna approached the man as though to shake hands with him. "All I had was fifteen dollars, but I put it in his hand. I'll tell you, . . . I could see tears in his eyes, because my husband already paid for the strawberries, and he gave him more than what he asked for." Anna laughs when she concludes this story. "My husband, when we got in the car, we're going down the road, he says: 'How much did you give him?'" (3–35, 36).

Anna's way of identifying Indians is identical to that of the strawberry seller. In a coffeeshop in Huntington Park, she spotted a young Indian man. She showed her husband how to identify Indians "through their nose and their cheekbones." Dean struck up a conversation with the young man, inviting him to have coffee with them. "So we got to talking. And my husband said: 'Are you, would you like something to eat?' Because they had just set our breakfast down, and [the young man] kept looking at my plate. . . . I felt sorry for him. . . . It just tears me to pieces. Here he had this coffee, and they kept filling it up. Well, you can't live on coffee like that for breakfast." Anna said to him, "Please don't think I'm forward, but, well, just order anything you want, . . . and I says, it's on us, o.k.?" The man did not respond. "He just gulped down his coffee. . . . Maybe he never had anybody ask him that before." Eventually they persuaded him to order breakfast. "He kept saying: 'Thank-you. Thank-you.'" After the young Indian explained that he was looking for work, Dean "pulled out some money . . . for the bus and to get something to eat." Anna relates: "It made my husband feel good, and he knew that I could have kissed him. Which I did" (3–38–41).

Although there appears to be a degree of ethnic cohesiveness involved, Anna attributes this beneficence to a family characteristic. "We more or less stick together that way, the few of us that's left. And we try to help each other, and if we feel we can do more, that's what we try to do. Most of them [the family members] feel that way" (3–42). When asked if she thinks this kind of beneficence is unique to her family or if other Indians would also have helped the young man, Anna replies: "Well, they probably would have. We naturally, one Indian can recognize another. . . . Whether they would help him or buy him food, they probably would, if they found out he didn't have anything or hadn't eaten" (3–42).

The family expresses confidence about the value of generosity. Patricia characterizes her maternal great-uncle, Elmer, as "a good person." When asked why she describes him in this way, Anna responds for her daughter: "He was always helping people. Giving 'em money to get something to eat. He couldn't stand to see anybody going hungry, and he'd do anything for you. If you called at three, four o'clock in the morning and told him you needed help, . . ." Pat finishes the sentence for her mother, "He was there" (4–5, 6).

KINSHIP AND FRIENDSHIP

Several scholars have noted that kinship and friendship are significant relationships for urban Indians.[7] In all of the stories thus far related by the Dawn family, none involve helping kin or friends. Although Anna reveals a preference for helping other Indians, she by no means excludes non-Indians as recipients of her beneficence. What she does insist on, though, is that the interaction be personal and immediate. When asked how she feels about giving money to organized charities, she emphatically replies: "No. I wouldn't do it that way" (5–19). Is this personal and immediate type of beneficence perhaps an urban expansion of the Indian kinship and friendship networks, which are shrinking? As Anna says, "The few of us that's left . . . try to help each other."

Another interpretation of the Dawn narratives of generosity toward virtual strangers is suggested by urban historian Oliver Zunz. "Ethnicity and class are two interwoven forces in American history and it may be artificial to try to separate them."[8]

PERCEPTIONS OF CLASS

When asked if people should share what they have, Patricia explicitly expresses an awareness of class distinctions in American society. "You mean the rich giving to the poor? Yeah. They [the rich] are always saying they want to do things [to help the poor], but I don't see 'em doing anything" (18–2).[9] Although American Indians may be perceived by scholars and by the general public as being among the poorest of the nation's poor, the Dawn family has not perceived itself in this manner, as evidenced by Pat's articulation of the family's attitude toward "poor people." She was told by her grandparents and parents: "You shouldn't look down your nose to them [poor people]. But don't be like them. Better yourself, but don't condemn them for being that way. Because it can't be helped" (2–64).

In American society, there is a long-standing moralistic attitude that poverty is the result of personal failings, such as drunkenness and laziness.[10] Significantly, this attitude is reflected in Pat's thinking. A clear change in the family's attitude is manifested when she continues: "To me, it can be helped. . . . You got too many people on welfare, taking my money that I'm working for, sitting back, doing nothing. I see it all the time. It just irritates me. I get mad when I walk into a store and they say, 'You got food stamps?' 'No,' I say, 'I work.' . . . I'm very, very dead set against that. You know, better yourself. Don't sit there on the couch all day drinking beer or having men coming in and out of your house or giving you money. Get out and get off your butt and work. Because I've always worked. Tracie's working, putting herself through school" (2–64, 65).

Tracie, although profoundly influenced by her grandparents, reveals the impact of Pat's perspective on her own thinking. She remembers her grandparents telling her: "A lot of people don't have a lotta money. They don't have food. They don't have clothing" (10–14). She says that she feels sorry for older people who are poor. "But these young guys, if they need money, . . . they're capable of getting a job. Some of them don't need to be asking for money" (10–15). She thinks that some people are lazy and don't deserve help. "These young people, they can go out and get a job. I don't feel one bit sorry for them. . . . They spend all their time getting drunk" (11–41).

The Dawn family, rather than feeling kinship with other poor groups in the city, apparently has identified with the classic concept of upward mobility: better yourself. Patricia and Tracie's identification with the working class is only suggested in these narrations, but their belief in the virtue of work is clearly articulated. An intriguing connection emerges between their beliefs and those of the traditional Cahuilla, who held that an industrious worker was a virtuous person, whereas a lazy individual was a disgrace.[11]

The strongest bond seems to be not with class, not with ethnicity, but with the elderly. Anna says, "A lot of them are in their eighties, you know, . . . and I want to help them any way I can" (5–8). All three women were moved by the plight of an elderly black man who was doing some work for Anna. "He's pretty sickly," says Anna. "I feel so darn sorry for him I could cry." She helps him clean the yard. "I don't want to see him do it." When she hears him coughing, she runs out to tell him: "Please go home. . . . You go home and rest. . . . By the way, would you like a sandwich?" Tracie says to Anna, "Oh, Grandma, poor thing, he's working and he's old." Then she asks if she can prepare coffee for him (7–33, 34).

Tracie's response to the frail old man is similar to Anna's: initial sympathy, then the desire to ease his discomfort with nourishment. It is a persistent pattern in the Dawn family. Their behavior expresses a belief in the virtue of respecting and helping elders. Because Tracie clearly emulates her grandmother, can the beneficence of this family be interpreted as an adherence to the values inculcated by the preceding generations?

ADHERENCE TO EARLIER TEACHINGS

Raymond C. White, in a study of Luiseño knowledge, explicates what he calls "common knowledge," which is contained in the term *hivikvitchi*. "Probably the bulk of Luiseño culture may be considered common knowledge. . . . [*Hivikvitchi*] may be translated as meaning 'the great knowledge of the ancients,' or as present-day common knowledge." A temporal ambiguity in the word does not exist for the Luiseño, White explains, "for the term also denotes continuity of culture."[12]

Continuity of culture, as manifested in generosity toward less fortunate people, is expressed by Anna. "[Generosity] has followed down through the generations, because, like I've said, everybody in the family has been that way. . . . People [non-Indians] think it's strange that everybody [in the family] would do the same things and have feelings in their heart to give" (3–15).

Anna recalls her parents "giving their last dollar" to someone in need. "My grandmother [Anna May Lawson Helm] was the same way. She would go out of her way to find out if there was a family that lived down the street that didn't have anything. She'd go give them money, and she'd also take them the best of meats. She always did. And milk, if they had kids. She'd get a lotta fruit and stuff and she'd take it . . . and knock on the door and then just leave the box" (1–44, 45).

When asked what her grandmother, Belva May Helm King, taught her, Pat replies without hesitation, "To help out when needed" (2–63). Tracie expresses what she has learned about beneficence from her family: "My grandmother and my mom share [with others]. Everybody in our family shares" (11–40). Articulating adherence to earlier teachings, Anna says: "I brought the kids up [to believe] it's always better to give than receive. That's what I taught them. My mother taught me. And I tried to teach my grandkids that too, you know. And my kids know it's always better to give than receive" (7–36). The expected continuity of this beneficence is evident in Tracie's narration. She plans to teach her own children that "it's a good thing to help" (10–18).

SUMMARY

The answers to the questions I have raised regarding the beneficence of the Dawn family are complex. The relative influences exerted on people's lives by inherited traditions, by the contemporary environment, and by new values and ideologies are not easily apportioned.[13] There does appear to be a persistence of traditional values, albeit in an altered form. In Cahuilla society, a well-balanced and rigidly enforced system of reciprocal relations operated at every level.[14] Although this system of reciprocity does not exist in Los Angeles in the 1990s, the interrelatedness of human beings and the resultant value placed on reciprocity are indicated in the narrations of these urban American Indian women. Reciprocal interactions are for this family, however, an abstract and amorphous concept: it is good to help those in need, and you may receive something in return, somehow, sometime.

The most clearly articulated traditional value that persists into the twentieth-century urban life of the Dawns is that of caring for the elderly. Tracie, spokesperson for the youngest generation, articulates this mentalité when she states that she would help someone in need but adds, "especially if they are elderly." The traditional value has undergone change in an urban milieu. In traditional society, the aged were protected and cared for to ensure that accumulated knowledge would be passed on to younger generations. Clearly, this function of beneficence to nonrelated elderly is not viable for the Dawns in Los Angeles. Why, then, does the value endure? Since there is no longer a tribal community of elders, are the Dawns perhaps seeking a surrogate community?

Identity with American Indians is clearly articulated in the narrations, but just as clear is the message that this family does not limit beneficence to kin and friends or even to Indians. Anna attests that if she sees someone in need, she helps, regardless of age and "regardless of the race or color." She explains, "I don't want to see anybody go hungry" (5–8). Because an Indian community does not exist for them in Los Angeles, are the Dawns unconsciously creating a surrogate community with a persistence in the traditional mentalité regarding beneficence?

Perhaps because of her own painful memories of poverty, Anna in her generosity makes no distinctions as to age or employability, whereas Patricia and Tracie express a change in mentalité regarding these distinctions. Beneficence in the Dawn family may be changing, as evidenced by Patricia and Tracie's belief that certain people are not deserving of generosity.[15] Any interpretation of this change in mentalité must take into account the upwardly mobile indoctrination by the older generations of Dawns in Los Angeles. They moved to the city because of opportunities to improve their economic condition, and this desire was undoubtedly conveyed to succeeding generations, together with the admonition "Better yourself."

Regarding not only upward mobility but virtually all aspects of mentalité, earlier teachings and personal relationships within the family are the significant determinants of the Dawn beneficence. Although Patricia and Tracie express an apparent change in their perception of who deserves help, the change may be only apparent, if one considers the Cahuilla dictum that a lazy person is a disgrace. Moreover, beneficent interactions are identical for all the Dawn women; the interactions are spontaneous, direct, and highly personalized. In this respect, each woman is who her mother taught her to be. A clue to the most viable interpretation of these stories of generosity lies, perhaps, in an awareness that reciprocity is only incidentally symmetrical.[16]

It is intriguing to discover that beneficence and reciprocity, intended to benefit the tribal community, persist in the city. Since the original community no longer exists, how can the persistence be interpreted? Although one cannot conclusively rule out the possibility that this beneficence is unique to the Dawn family, I believe that the Dawns are following an ancient tradition by finding self-fulfillment and self-expression in giving. As Anna says: "I don't do it for glory" (1–43). "It does make me feel good when I do something like that" (1–45). The urban shift in this mentalité, extending beneficence to a nontribal group, is not an atrophy, not a loss of culture, but a dynamic adaptation to change, one that allows continuity of a central dimension of Cupeño ethos.

CHAPTER 5

THE METAPHYSICAL REALM

Tu'uyu: *Cupan for "to dream"*

One day, before I could set up the tape recorder, Anna began talking about her dream of the previous night. Although I had planned to interview her on a different topic, I asked: "Do you want to talk about that, Anna? About your dreams?" She expressed a need to tell me about the dream, and this narration opened a new area of investigation, that of the metaphysical realm.

It's just that we're all together, the family. . . . We're all talking, and we're eating dinner together. And everybody's just smiling. . . . I can just see my dad, and he was always calling me "Honey." . . . I can just hear him say: "Honey, would you do me a favor?" And I said, "Yeah, Dad." And my husband, it's his face, and yet it's not his face. It's his body. . . . He's my husband, [but] he don't look the same, in my dream. Like I said, my husband was a very, very handsome man. But he's got his hair parted down the middle, which my husband never did do. . . . It's my uncle's hair, 'cause my uncle parted his hair down the middle. There's just different things on him, and yet it's him. [In the dream] my grandmother's hair, it's not white. She used to [when she was] younger dye it black, you know. I mean she had black hair but she dyed it black-black. . . . In my dream she's got that black-black hair. And she just is smiling. She don't say much to me. In fact, hardly anybody talks. I'm the one doing most of the talking in there to them. Just asking how they are. And yet I know they're gone, you know what I mean? It's strange. (16–1, 2)

She continues this narration by repeating that her father is asking her to do something for him, but it is not a real conversation. She attributes the dream to the fact that she and Patricia and Tracie had recently visited the family graves. "We took flowers out and cleaned the graves up. Cleaned them all up and polished them. Maybe it's because I was saying: 'Oh, I've missed you so much.' Maybe that's why they keep coming back into my dream" (16–2).

Although the Dawn narrations of metaphysical experiences may not appear as necessarily Indian, I suggest that these experiences reveal emergent forms of tribal beliefs onto which non-Indian practices have been grafted. Anna's narration of her dream illustrates the belief of Swedish scholar Åke Hultkrantz regarding the supernatural in American Indian thinking. "The continuous, expected process of everyday reality is disrupted by the supernatural reality with its discontinuous, unexpected, and, above all, incomprehensible course of events."[1] Several times during the narration, Anna says, "It's so strange."

Hultkrantz attributes the lack of words for *religion* in American Indian languages to the phenomenon that religious values and attitudes permeated life in these cultures and did not exist in isolation from other cultural manifestations. Not only shamans but also ordinary people perceived their dreams as passageways into the spirit world. Dreams and visions are the means by which Indians can access the sources of power, which are ability and knowledge.[2]

PRECONTACT PERCEPTIONS OF THE SUPERNATURAL

Because of this integration of the natural and the supernatural, of the mundane and the sacred, whites have previously perceived American Indians as having no religion. "Time is scarcely remote," Hultkrantz reminds us, "when white people thought there were tribes without religion in America."[3] In 1822 the Franciscan priest Jeronimo Boscana wrote that the Indians were "so ignorant, without being able to distinguish the true from the false, [that] they did not know the path of light, and continually walked in darkness." Arguing that the Mission Indians were materialists because they did not distinguish soul from body, he expressed his belief that they "did not believe one way or the other" regarding the immortality of the soul. He added, "For what they say is that thus the ancients did, and that they are doing the same as they learned from their ancestors."[4]

Although the pioneering anthropologist Stephen Powers complained that it was the California Indians' "melancholy fate" to be so little understood, he himself made a dubious contribution to the scholarship when he wrote in 1877 about their "ignorance." He stated, "I am thoroughly convinced that a great majority of the California Indians had no conception whatever of a Supreme Being." He argued that any concept these Indians had of God(s) was "manifestly a modern graft upon their ideas."[5] Hultkrantz refutes scholars' interpretation that the Californian image of a deity reflects missionary influence.[6]

The spiritual expressions and belief systems of American Indians are much more profound than their depiction in ethnography, which for southern

Above:
Schoolhouse on Pechanga Indian Reservation, in front of graveyard

Below:
Graveyard at Pechanga Indian Reservation, where Steve Helm is buried

California Indians is particularly scant and vague. Regarding the Cahuilla specifically, Kroeber states, "Regrettably little is known of their religion." He documents Cupeño religion only briefly and exclusively in terms of ritual ceremonies, including the *toloache* initiation ceremony. Toloache (jimsonweed or datura), a plant with dramatic narcotic properties, was used in California for ritual and medicinal purposes.[7]

A religious subsystem that developed out of the toloache cult among several tribes in southern California was the *Chinigchinich* religion. Scholars have theorized that this religion developed as the result of contact with whites, since many of its central features appear to reflect Christian themes. C. G. DuBois describes Chinigchinich as having "a distinct and difficult rule of life, requiring obedience, fasting, and self-sacrifice. It had the sanction of fear, . . . and above all it had the seal of inviolable secrecy."[8]

None of the Dawn women had heard of either the toloache cult or the Chinigchinich variation. Patricia's response is representative: "Is it [toloache] like loco weed? . . . As long as they use it for that [religious purposes] and don't abuse it, I think it's great. . . . But it has to be an elder doing it. I don't know if the young ones [know what they are doing]" (14–21).

Franciscan Father Geronimo Boscana, in attempting to describe the beliefs of the southern California Indians, observed that the "deity" Chinigchinich was known by three sacred names: Saor, common person; Quoar, the most sacred; and Tobet, medicine man.[9] In his fieldwork among California Indians, John Harrington refers to Tobet: "California bush rabbit. This tiny rabbit was the first man who ever sang in the world."[10] Anna's grandfather gave Patricia the nickname "Little Tobet," telling her it meant "Little Rabbit" (2–10). Although one cannot identify it as a remnant of a cult belief, the nickname "Tobet" has an intriguing resonance.

The inviolable secrecy to which DuBois refers has been noted by other observers. Father Boscana complained, "It is difficult to penetrate their [religious] secrets."[11] Raymond White, authority on Luiseño beliefs, interprets this phenomenon, "Secrecy, strategem, and dissimulation are bound up with the concept that religious knowledge, formula, and ceremony possess power."[12] A similar secrecy is dramatically manifested in the Dawn life histories. Anna relates her grandfather's experiences with religion. "My grandfather didn't . . . stay on religion very long. . . . You didn't ask him why, how come, or anything else. When he said that's it, that's it. You didn't come back and say: 'Well, how come this? How come that?' You didn't. . . . When he said that was enough, that was enough" (5–33–34). Anna continues: "A lot of his friends were Catholic. And he'd say, he'd never join that, he always called them a communist club. . . . He said: '[They] go out and drink and then run and confess.' He didn't believe in that. He said when you do wrong, you just don't run over to confess to somebody and say: 'I did this,' and then come right back and go into the bar" (5–32–33).

Anna recalls that her grandfather accompanied her grandmother to a Baptist or Methodist church. "When we'd get after him and tell him he should go to church, . . . he'd say he didn't need church" (5–34). "He never really questioned anybody . . . what religion do you belong to? . . . He never asked anybody, and he sure didn't want anybody asking him. He'd say: 'That's my business. I know what I am.' That's the way my grandfather was. . . . He didn't want nobody prying into his life. . . . when they, being nosy, asked him what religion, . . . a lotta times he'd say: 'What the hell difference does it make? I'm here, aren't I?' [Then] he'd walk off" (7–47).

When Steve "Box" Helm died, and the family was preparing the funeral arrangements, Anna vividly remembers that it was "such a shock" to discover that he had converted to Catholicism (7–43). "I don't know who talked him into becoming a Catholic, . . . because we were Methodist or Baptist. . . . Whichever church we wanted to go to, it was one of them. And that's why we couldn't understand why and when he had done it. And without telling my [grandmother or my] mother" (7–44). Anna reports that her mother was furious when she discovered Steve Helm's secret. As the family was driving at night to the church to view the body, "all the lights in the car went out." Anna remembers: "We blew a tire. . . . That was the weirdest feeling. . . . My mother and I thought the same thing, that it was because she was mad because grandfather had gone Catholic. . . . Maybe he was trying to put it in her mind: 'I'll show you!'" (5–29).

Belva May, Anna's mother, had another occasion at a later date to be similarly furious. When Tracie was about four years old, she "let it slip about going to [Catholic] communion." Anna says, "When my mother found out, she just flipped her lid" (7–45). Like her great-grandfather, Patricia had secretly converted to Catholicism and taken Tracie with her. Anna remembers: "My mother jumped all over me 'cause she thought I knew about it. [But] I said: 'She what?!' I didn't know she'd done that. So that was a sore subject. My mother wouldn't speak to my daughter for quite a while" (7–46).

Although both identify themselves as Catholic, neither Patricia nor Tracie attend church anymore. Tracie reports that the last time she went to church was in February 1988, the weekend after her grandfather died. "I just sat in there and prayed for him and lit a candle" (11–39). Although she derived comfort from this visit to church, she states that she and her mother have quit attending mass because the churches in their area have only Spanish-language services (11–40). Patricia confirms this: "I don't go to church. I haven't been to church in years." She attributes this change to her coming to agree with her grandmother that the Catholic church was "a money-hungry religion that didn't care about people" (14–16).

Anna May, like her husband, Steve Helm, had her own religious secrets. A devoted follower of the evangelist preacher Oral Roberts, she wore a particular piece of cloth at all times. Pat remembers discovering Anna May Lawson's secret. "I didn't know she wore it, until I had gone in to see if she was okay one night. And I seen this thing pinned to her nightgown. I asked her what it was for, and she said: 'I always have it with me.' And then I found out she wore it on her slip. She never took it off, . . . except when she was bathing" (14–15). Pat adds: "To me, it looked like a little piece of dirty cloth. But that was hers, and she'd kept that with her at all times" (14–14, 15).[13] Patricia reports that "Gram" evidently believed it possessed power, and she was very secretive about it.

Secrecy is integrally related to the concept that religious knowledge possesses power. Several scholars, notably White and Bean, have observed widely shared concepts of power in the world views of southern California Indians. White refers to the Luiseño term *ayelkwi*. "The Luiseño render this concept into English with the term 'knowledge,' although 'knowledge-power' would approach it more closely." Power was believed to be ubiquitous and continually available.[14] When asked if he has observed any vestige of the concept of ayelkwi in his parish, a past rector of Mission San Antonio de Pala responded: "Yes, I find this with a few older men in the community. They don't just see a bird, they invest it with profound meaning."[15]

Dreaming and calling on power sources were among the means through which power might be acquired. Moreover, power could be tapped through many other channels.[16] A vivid recollection for Anna is the power in her mother's and grandmother's healing hands. "My mother had healing in her hands. She would rub her hands, and I'd go lay down on the bed. [But] I would say, okay, just for a couple of minutes, Mom. And she would go in there and she would rub and rub her hands together, and then she'd put them on [me], and I could feel all that tingling from her hands going into my body. But when she got through, it would make her so weak. That's why I didn't want her to do it. It took all her power out of her body. . . . She would get weak as a kitten. She'd break out in a sweat, and, that's why I didn't want her doing it" (6–6). She remembers that her grandmother had more power in her hands than her mother and that both would heal with their hands only when it was really needed. "I remember when I was a little kid [people] would come over and tell them that their arm hurt, or their back hurt, or leg hurt. And they'd want my mother [to heal them]" (6–7). Whenever Anna had a severe headache, either Belva May or Anna May would place her hands on Anna's forehead and on the back of Anna's head. "They had to do it two to three times, in order to get the headache. But you could feel the tingling go through you. Through your whole body" (7–15).

Among California Indians, it was believed that as power is distributed differentially and hierarchically throughout the universe, so is it distributed among human beings. Certain individuals are naturally born with power or inherit it.[17] In the Dawn family, apparently, it was only the women who manifested healing power, although Anna has not inherited it. She explains her grandmother's and her mother's healing powers thus: "They were just gifted. . . . God just put [the power] in their body, and they worked it out that way. It's strange, but I'll tell you, it did work" (7–16).

Anna also talks about a power not commonly thought of as being Indian, that of her grandmother's ability to successfully conduct seances. "Moving the table" is a power that Anna believes she inherited from her grandmother through her mother. Anna was about nine years old when she began to participate in the seances (6–5). She relates that it was usually only women who would take part (7–1). She describes how a seance works:

To begin with, you just all hold hands. . . . I'll tell them who I'm going to try to contact. Then they have to concentrate, whether they know [the person to be contacted] or not. When I say, like, it'd be my husband, then they have to put that in their mind: it's my husband, and his name is Dean. So you just concentrate and concentrate. . . . Then the table will start moving. . . . I'll say: "Is this you, Dean?" . . . [But] if my mother's mind was stronger than my husband's she would enter. . . . I've seen other minds take over that way. . . . That's why you gotta ask: "Is this you, Dean? Or Gram?" . . . They want to get through to let you know that it's them, and they're alright. . . . The table would move . . . once for no and two for yes. And like I'll say: "Is that you, Mom?" If it don't move, then I have to keep saying: "Is this you, Gram?" or "Is this you, Elmer?" Or Meredith or Kenneth or Dad. . . . You just go through the whole thing, until finally the table [moves]. (7–3, 4)

When asked whom she has contacted through seances, Anna responds: "We used to contact my aunts and uncles . . . and my grandfather. . . . We just asked him if he was happy. He said: 'Yes.' And if he had seen his friend, Mr. Cook, who had passed on. And this friend's wife. And he'd say: 'Yes.' And [we asked] if he had seen Tottie . . . his son that died when he was little. And he'd just answer: 'Yes' to pretty near everything. . . . It may sound silly, but a lotta times you get a pretty good feeling" (7–4, 5). The degree to which the spirits of loved ones are integrated into daily lives is suggested by these questions asked during the seance: "Are you with us all the time? Was that you that made the door open?" Anna relates that her grandfather would answer yes to these questions but no to the question, "You don't want us to forget you?" (7–6).

Anna explains what happens when she suggests during the seance that the spirit is with them at that moment. "Sometimes, that table, honest to God, I'm not exaggerating, that table really shakes, especially if they want to get something over to the question that you asked them. . . . And man, that table has really, really rocked. . . . One time my brother asked my grandfather . . . 'Pop, are you in hell?' And man, that table raised up! I'll tell you, that thing shook, and . . . it scared my brother so bad. . . . Evidently . . . my grandfather didn't like what he said, and that table, honest to God, . . . you could hear the legs just pounding. . . . That was the last time my brother ever said anything to anybody about doing a seance" (7–6, 7).

When asked if a seance is ever not successful, Anna replies: "It takes a lot of concentration. You can't have nothing blocking your mind. . . . And a lot of people have other thoughts come in. . . . It breaks the spirit, you know, . . . that's trying to get through to you. . . . Sometimes thoughts get to you other than the person you want to talk to" (7–7, 8). Anna talks about what happens if there is somebody in the group who really doesn't believe and is just fooling around. "That's why it takes so long sometimes [to contact a spirit]. . . . You just have to ask them to leave, if they're not going to be serious" (7–18).

What benefit does Anna derive from conducting seances? "It makes me happy, knowing that I can get through to them and talk to them and ask them different things, like if they're happy. It just makes me feel good knowing I can get in contact with them. It really does. It just gives you a real excitement. I mean I can feel my body just tingling when I'm trying to talk to them. . . . I can just feel. I know they're close. . . . Just knowing that I can do something like that, with the power" (9–2, 3).

Although power was also perceived as potentially dangerous, in Cahuilla belief the *tewlavilem*, the souls that had a separate existence after death, passed messages on to the living, advising and aiding those still on earth.[18] In this particular area of the metaphysical realm, that of communicating with the dead, the Dawn women exhibit no fear. They perceive the spirits of their deceased loved ones as helpful and powerful friends.

COMMUNICATING WITH THE DEAD

One night Anna was folding clothes in her bedroom. "My husband came to me, right in front of the bed. . . . I happened to look up and there he was. And he was just smiling. I mean, honest to God. I looked up, something made me look up. . . . There his face was, . . . just smiling, as if to say: 'Oh, I'm so happy, you know. And I looked at him, and I says: 'Okay, honey. Okay, honey, I know you're happy.' When I looked again, he was smiling, but his face was just fading. I mean it was like smoke. And he's come to me two or three times that way. . . . When he appears, he's smiling" (5–36).

Patricia reports that she feels "very comfortable" with the spirit of her grandmother in her house. "I get up in the middle of the night and walk around. And I know she's back there. She's not going to hurt me" (14–11). She recognizes that the spirit is her grandmother because of an odor she detects. "She had a perfume she would wear. . . . And every once in a while that'll go by my nose. It's very strong, and I know she's there. And I talk to her. . . . I think she's done something to let me know she's there. . . . One night we were sitting in the front room watching TV, and my kitchen light went on, and there was nobody in there." Pat laughs at the recollection, "I got up, and I said: 'Grandma, knock it off'" (14–11).

She also reports that things mysteriously move from where they were placed. "Things move. Her spirit's back there [in the house], and I'm glad. . . . I have a picture of my dad, my grandmother, and my great-grandmother by my bed. And I always talk to them. I'll walk in, and I'll sit down and I'll go: 'Hi, group.' And I'll tell them what happened that day, . . . just like they're alive. They can understand what I'm saying." When asked what messages the spirits have for her, Pat responds that her grandmother would say, "Behave." Her father would say, "Be happy." Both are messages she finds comforting.

Tracie has identical responses to questions about fearing the spirits in her life. She feels that her grandfather is not going to hurt them and that her great-grandmother "just wanted to check up" on them, to see if they were "okay." Tracie adds, "I know she's not going to hurt us" (11–3).

There appears to be no change over these three generations regarding a fear of the deceased. There is, however, a fear that is articulated by Tracie and that is not manifested in the narrations of Anna or Patricia. "I was scared to death of dying," Tracie relates. "I would lay awake at night, sometimes watching TV, trying to force my eyes open, because I was scared of dying" (11—36). She reveals that she has "always had a fear" but that it became acute when her beloved grandfather was terminally ill. She reports that the fear "is better now," since she talked to her grandmother and mother. She also seems to have absorbed some of Patricia's belief that the life hereafter is a happy one. Pat attributes this belief to Dean Dawn. "My dad was the type that didn't believe in mourning. He hated that. . . . He said that [the deceased] are ten times better than you or I. . . . They're not hurting. They're not in poverty" (14—13).

It is reasonable to assume that Tracie's fear may be an individual response to the painful and prolonged deaths, from cancer, of both her grandfather and her great-grandfather. One cannot, on the other hand, entirely rule out a vestigal fragment of the distant tribal past. "The impress of death is heavy on the mind of the California Indian," states Kroeber. "He thinks of it, speaks of it, . . . weeps unrestrainedly when the recollection of his dear ones makes him think of his own end. He wails for days for his kin."[19]

It must be noted, though, that Anna Dawn's family appears to be atypical of Kroeber's description of California Indians in mourning. She describes the mourners at her grandfather's funeral: "Indians don't cry at the services. . . . Everyone, . . . all the women, the men, they moaned a little bit, but they didn't cry" (17—6). During the funeral for her husband, who died on February 16, 1988, Anna was crying for a time. Then, she recalls: "I don't know what happened. . . . Here I was crying. I know they could hear me. . . . I know everyone could hear me. Then, just like that, a vision of a big cloud came over me, and I just stopped. . . . I didn't want them to see me crying. . . . I haven't cried since" (17–8). Anna attributes this phenomenon in part to her relief from "knowing that he went to a better place" (17–7).

The belief in a life hereafter, according to Hultkrantz, was firmly established among native peoples before contact, and statements to the contrary "should be considered with reservation."[20] It appears likely, however, that Anna's belief that her husband went to a better place reflects a Christian influence. Ethnographers have recorded American Indians' complex concepts regarding an afterlife, none of which precisely equate with the Christian concept of heaven and hell.

Anthropologist Ruth Underhill, former Supervisor of Indian Education, U.S. Indian Service, finds a belief in spirits and a purposeful attempt to conciliate them in every Indian tribe. "It was thought that the average dead person existed in the afterworld only until the last person who remembered him on earth was gone."[21] Anna believes that visits from the spirits of deceased family members are primarily due to their longing to be remembered.

Bean describes the *telmikis*, the afterlife of the Cahuilla, as being the land lying to the east of Cahuilla territory, which was home to those who had died. "Entrance to this land was not automatic — or easy."[22] The spirits of the Luiseño, according to White, "are disconsolate over the loss of immortality and reluctant to leave the region of their lifetime attachment."[23]

The spirits of the Dawn loved ones, though perhaps not disconsolate, appear reluctant to depart. During an interview in January 1989, Anna related that her father, who had died in July of the previous year, had been on her mind constantly. "I don't know if he's trying to tell me something. . . . It's like he didn't get a chance to tell me what he wanted me to know. . . . It's that grin of his. But I don't know if he's trying to tell me that he's happy, or if he's trying to tell me that he didn't get to finish what he was going to tell me" (3–16, 17). "There's something that I haven't done or I was supposed to do and didn't do it" (5–39). When asked what her father's message to her might be, she responds: "I have not the faintest idea. But it's something that he didn't get a chance to talk to me [about], because I can't get him out of my mind. I cannot get my dad out of my mind" (5–35).

Regarding the spirit of her husband, however, she says: "It's strange. My husband has come to me [and] just smiles, [to] let me know that everything's all right. And I still see him, not his body, just his face" (5–35). The Cahuilla tewlavil appeared frequently to the living in various forms, sometimes as a visual image. More often this "soul spirit" appeared in dreams or manifested its presence in some other way, such as a draft of air, an odor, or in the thoughts of the living.[24] "Most Luiseño ghosts tend to remain in the vicinity," notes White. "As ghosts and individualists they are removed from ordinary social controls, but are still able to exercise *ayelkwi*. This makes them so dangerous that final banishment is necessary."[25]

The Dawns reveal no need to banish their "ghosts." On the contrary, they find them comforting. "Like I said," Anna repeats, "I know they won't hurt me. . . . Since my mother knew that I could make the table move, I think that's what she's trying to tell me. She wants me to get in contact to talk to them. That's the way I'm feeling" (16–15). She believes the proper way to achieve this communication is through a seance. "That's why I asked Patricia if she'd like to have a seance." Pat's response was an enthusiastic "Yes!" (16–10). "I would love to do that" (14–28). Anna describes her feelings on a recent evening when she felt the power to move the table. "I had so much power in my hands, . . . like I had the strength of twenty people [in] my fingers. . . . That's how my mind has been lately" (16–11). During the course of this narration, she paused at one point and checked my reaction by asking, "Do you think I'm cracking up?"

Anna's concern that I might think she is cracking up when she relates these metaphysical experiences is understandable. From the time of contact with white society, the religious perceptions of native Californians were ridiculed as stories of delirium or, worse, deliberate deceits. Father Boscana wrote in 1822: "It is easily recognized that their reports on the immortality of the soul are nothing more than fabulous stories and lies for deceiving the simple, . . . and how slight must be their belief in the spiritual substance with which we are adorned, and this not only on the part of the rudest and most ignorant ones of them, but on the part of those most versed and best instructed in our holy religion."[26]

POSTCONTACT PERCEPTIONS OF THE SUPERNATURAL

With the emphasis in the eighteenth and nineteenth centuries on saving the souls of tribal peoples by changing their religion, Europeans believed that they were destroying false religion, whereas in reality they were destroying a total moral and ethical system.[27] This destruction was particularly traumatic for the Cupeño, who were removed from their homelands.[28]

The acceptance of Christianity did not mean that native religious systems disappeared. Noting that California Indians did not surrender their metaphysical concepts to Christianity, Sherburne Cook states that there is no reason to assume, on the other hand, that these Indians did not add Christian concepts to their own system of beliefs. Native religious ceremonies persisted alongside Catholicism and were often tolerated by the priests under the guise of secular events, though sometimes carried out secretly.[29]

Illustrating this phenomenon, DuBois described a Mission Indian fiesta at Mesa Grande at the turn of the century. Religious worship was the most important aspect of the fiesta, with an Indian youth acting as acolyte during the mass and serving "reverently about the altar." The chant *Santo, Santo*, led by an old Indian woman named Angela, raised "a thin volume of sound upon the summer air." When the long services were over, the secular pleasures of the fiesta began. It had not been planned to present Indian dances, for the priest had "long discouraged these reminders of barbarism." A few white guests, however, bribed the dancers. An old woman, whose earliest religious ritual included the Indian dance, threw her heart and soul into her singing. DuBois wrote: "In the rapt expression of her dusky face there is no hint of the gentle ecstasy which filled Angela's eyes as she sang the *Santo*. . . . An artist should have painted the one as the Christian, the other as the pagan sibyl."[30]

The former rector of Mission San Antonio de Pala articulated his thinking on this issue:

For them [Indians in the parish] religion is different from what we want to define. . . . The true religion is only this one, that

Christ came to teach, which is true. But for those who didn't know, or for those who have a different education, we have to respect their own view of God.... Only God can judge them.... If I see a native living differently, I have to have respect, because if he sees a different God, I have to be careful not to destroy [his] belief so that he doesn't have anything to believe in.... We have, as the church does now, to take a different attitude than the first missionaries who went in and said: "We have the true God. This is the God you must accept." Maybe they were not able to see something good, positive in native [beliefs]. (22–4, 5)

Telling the Dawn women about a Catholic priest in Los Angeles who is also an Ojibway medicine man, I questioned them about his practice of including Indian drum music and purification ceremonies in the celebration of the mass.[31] Tracie responded that she would find such an integration confusing (11–11). Anna asked, "Are they really Indians that go there?" When told that the priest evidently is really an Indian, she expressed a mild interest in visiting the church. "I wouldn't mind seeing what they're doing" (12–19).

Most southern California Mission Indians are practicing Roman Catholics but retain an attenuated form of their precontact religion. The Indian graveyard at Pala is notable for the personal possessions and gifts on top of the graves.[32] The priests of the Pala mission have observed this practice. One of the priests acknowledges that the objects, such as an eagle feather, were appreciated by the deceased in life, but he seems puzzled by the ritual. He can understand placing a doll on the grave of a child, but sometimes "a wife puts boots" (22–9).

Father Xavier Colleoni, rector of Mission San Antonio de Pala, estimates that 98 percent of his parish is Catholic; the other religions represented include Jehovah's Witnesses and the Church of Jesus Christ of Latter-day Saints. "Some people have started their own church," reports Father Colleoni, "which is involved primarily in Bible study."[33]

Patricia talks about her grandparents' involvement with evangelical religion. "I call it a holy-roller church. . . . I went a couple of times. . . . They were rolling on the floor and screaming Hallelujah. It scared the hell out of me the first time. . . . And on Sunday mornings, my grandmother always had Oral Roberts on TV. . . . My great-grandmother had on [TV] her little Jimmy Swaggert. . . . My grandfather would have whoever was on TV, but he did like Jimmy Swaggert. In fact, one time when they had a TV special, [my grandparents] were in the audience" (14–17, 18, 19). Patricia's evaluation of these evangelical preachers reveals a distinct change in attitude. She notes, "I think they're phony" (14–19). During the time her great-grandparents and her grandparents were following TV evangelists and attending an Assembly of God church, they were also occasionally visiting an "Indian church" in the area. How Steve Helm managed to attend Catholic mass as well is a mystery.

Anna's narration provides the most details on the Indian church. She found out about the church from a throwaway newspaper in which there was a notice that the reverend welcomed American Indians. Anna's family attended several times, and Anna "loved the way they sing. They do a lot of singing" (5–21). The family became disenchanted with the church, however, because the minister was continually "harping on drinking" (5–25). "I just got tired of him preaching on drinking. [He preached] Indians are drunk. Indians don't hold a job. They're drunk all the time. They don't show up for work" (5–26). Moreover, the reverend was believed to be a non-Indian and had a reputation for abusing alcohol. Anna thought the minister was treating the Indians in his congregation like "bad little kids, . . . like he was the big chief" (5–27).

Neither Anna nor Patricia remembers the name of the church, but evangelical churches, many located in the South Gate, Bellflower, and Huntington Park areas of Los Angeles, have been more assertive than mainstream religions in creating ethnic-oriented ministries. Jonathan Wilson, a Choctaw and minister of the First Indian Baptist Church in South Gate, estimates that fewer than 1 percent of Indian people in Los Angeles go to church on Sunday. He tells his congregation, "To be a Christian, you don't stop being Indian." Wilson is wary, however, of using Indian symbolism in Christian worship. "You have to be very careful, because Indians associate culture with their religion."[34]

The ethnographic literature on California Indians documents the integration of religion and culture. A widely shared fundamental concept was the belief that knowledge, and therefore power, could be achieved through dreaming and visions.[35]

DREAMS AND VISIONS

Spirits come unbidden during Anna's dreams, but since she is puzzled about the messages they have for her, she is considering conducting a seance. "I've been dreaming about them every night. They're in my dreams, . . . all at the same time. . . . That's the first time . . . we were all together. Other times, it's been just my husband or my mother or my grandmother . . . my uncles . . . in there with my dad. . . . It's related to the whole family, the ones that passed away. I've been thinking strongly. Maybe that's why I . . . want to do the table, . . . give a seance. . . . Maybe they want me to go ahead and ask questions. . . . It's just something that's causing me to dream of my parents and my husband every night, and my grandparents" (16–5, 6).

She believes there is a message trying to get through. "I get that feeling like they're trying to tell me something, . . . and I don't know what it is. . . . It's been bothering me. What is it about my husband? I know he wants me to be happy. . . . He won't let anything hurt the family. . . . I don't know what it is. It's something there. I've never [dreamed] this way before, this long" (16–7). As of this writing, however, Anna has not conducted the seance, stating that she feels conditions have not been right for the degree of concentration required.

In discussing the concept of tradition and authority in the Cahuilla world view, Bean states, "The past was a reference point for the present and future."[36] Anna appears to be seeking a reference point from the past in the following dream: "[I'm] looking in the mirror. It's my body, but I can't see my face in the mirror. There's no face at all" (16–7). "I'm trying so hard to look in that mirror to see what my mother's doing to my hair. When I was a little kid, she'd say: 'Wash your hair, honey.' . . . [In the dream] she's trying to roll it, and I didn't want it rolled, because she rolled it too tight. And I tried to tell her. . . . She said: 'You're my little girl. You're still my little girl.' . . . I couldn't see my face in the mirror to see what she was doing. I could feel it, but I couldn't see it" (16–9).

The distinction between past and present is erased in dreams. There is frequently a warm and loving merging of the dream world and the conscious waking world in Anna's narrations. Her dreams are no different from her waking thoughts about her family. "During the night," she relates, "I get a cup of coffee, and I sit here and I think . . . of the good tims that I went through with my family and how fortunate I was to have such a beautiful family. . . . It's real quiet, . . . and it makes me feel good knowing that I said: 'Goodnight, Gram,' or 'Goodnight, Mom,' or 'Goodnight, honey'" (16–12).

Dreams can be prospective as well as retrospective. During April 1989, Anna's home was burglarized; the only items stolen were her Indian jewelry. Two nights before the theft, she dreamed of her father. "I remember that my dad was trying to, he was smiling at me, and he was trying to tell me something about the Indians. Now that's all I could get out of him, the Indian. Now whether he meant the Indian jewelry, I don't know. . . . [But I did think:] 'Well, I'll put it away. . . . No big hurry. I'll put it away tomorrow.' . . . My dad was trying to tell me. He just kept saying: 'Indian.' . . . I said: 'O.K., Dad. O.K., Dad, I will.' . . . I could just kick myself, I'll tell you, for not [putting the jewelry away]" (17–2).

Sometimes the tewlavil asked the living to join it, so it would not be lonely, and sometimes expressed displeasure that the mourning rituals had not been properly carried out or personal property not taken care of.[37] Anna worries about whether she has taken care of her father's personal business as he would have wished. She often makes a connection between her dreams and visions and her visits to the cemetery. "Maybe it [the dreaming] is because I haven't been out to the cemetery, I don't know. It's something involved with my family, and I haven't been out there. . . . I used to go every week, . . . but I haven't been [lately]. Maybe that's what they're telling me. . . . In my mind, they're telling me I don't care anymore. They're forgotten. So maybe all this [dreaming] boils down to that one thing, that I haven't been out there [to the graves], and they're reminding me in my dreams" (17–2).

A dramatic story about a spirit who expresses displeasure is told by Anna. Because Anna was scheduled to check into the hospital for surgery, a friend invited her to go shopping to cheer her up. While Anna was admiring a dress, "navy blue with polka dots," the face of her Aunt Florence appeared on the dress. "It was just a big flash of her face, and she wasn't smiling or nothin'." Anna's friend, noticing her distress, asked what was troubling her. Anna replied, "I just seen my aunt." The friend, looking around, asked, "Where?" When Anna replied that she had seen her aunt's face on the polka-dot dress, her friend attributed the vision to Anna's anxiety about impending surgery. But Anna insisted: "I'm telling you, my aunt's face was on the dress. . . . Why would it come to me on this dress?" When she arrived home, the vision bothered her so much she phoned her mother and learned that Aunt Florence had just died (5–44, 45).

In the hospital, awaiting surgery, Anna was lying in bed, which was facing a blank wall. "All of a sudden, . . . my aunt's face, just as big as you please, appeared on that wall, and she was smiling. Now, on the dress she wouldn't smile. But on the wall, she was smiling. . . . She was smiling, but it wasn't a full smile. . . . I was in the hospital when they had the [funeral] services, so I couldn't go" (5–45, 46). Since her aunt's face had appeared twice in the same day and was not smiling in the first vision, Anna interpreted the visions as an expression of her aunt's displeasure. "I was going to visit her in the hospital. . . . And, see, I didn't get a chance. I said [to the vision]: 'Oh, Aunt Florence, I'm sorry I didn't get to visit you, [and] I'm not going to be able to go to the funeral, because I have to be in here [in the hospital]'" (5–47). She interpreted the second vision, the slightly smiling one, as her aunt's acceptance of her apology.

Rather than feeling she is visited by lonely or neglected spirits, Patricia believes that her dreams about deceased relatives are the result of her unwillingness to let go of the people she loves so much. "For a long time, just like with my dad, I couldn't let [my grandmother] go. I used to dream my grandmother was in the front room in a coffin, in my house. And that's because I wouldn't let her go. . . . For a long time [after my grandmother's death], I wouldn't accept the fact that she wasn't here anymore. And I used to dream about her being in a coffin in my living room. For a long time, I was still holding onto her. . . . Every once in a while, I'll [still] have [the dream], and she'll be in there. But she'll be with my dad and my great-grandmother" (14–10). She derives comfort from the dreams in which Anna May Helm is with the other spirits and also from the belief that her great-grandmother is present in her life. As noted previously, she frequently perceives this presence through "certain smells, . . . perfumes, certain colognes that she used to love to wear. Every once in a while, it'll whiff by my nose. I don't wear it, and my mom doesn't wear it, so I know she's back there [in my house]" (18–1).

Although Tracie does not recall having similar dreams, she is aware of spirits in the house. She hears the footsteps of "Gram" Anna May on the uncarpeted surfaces of the house. She is not afraid of this spirit, nor is she concerned about messages her great-grandmother may have for her (11–3, 4). "Because, see, my [great-]grandmother passed away when I was young" (11–5). Tracie was about five years old when Anna May Helm died and ten years old when her great-grandmother, Belva May Helm, died in 1979.

Frequently in Anna's dreams, "Gram is doing all the cooking." Anna says: "We were crazy about her cooking and her apple pies. And Mom's helping her, . . . and Dad's telling the jokes, making them all laugh" (16–17). Although Patricia and Tracie appear to have similar loving feelings about their deceased relatives, they report dreams less often than Anna. However, Patricia's dreams will sometimes coincide with those of her mother.

The most recent visits by the spirit of Dean Dawn occurred on the same evening. Both Anna and Pat had nearly identical dreams in which they ask Dean, "Where have you been?" Pat's dream was so vivid that when she awoke, she immediately went to her mother's house, convinced she would find Dean sitting in the kitchen. One distinction between Anna's and Patricia's dreams was the way in which Dean was dressed. In Pat's dream, he was wearing his bib overalls, which she remembers as his favorite attire at home, whereas Anna was struck by the elegance of his dress in her dream. He was wearing a silk shirt, with shoes to match. Puzzled, Anna declares, "He doesn't even like silk shirts." Both Anna and Patricia report that Dean came to reassure them and to tell them that he would be back from time to time.

In her autobiography, the Diegeño Delfina Cuero expresses her belief that there are two kinds of dreams, good and bad, both sent by "witches." Dreams represent profound power, but she says, "Nobody dreams power like that anymore."[38] Evidently, the Dawn family can still dream power, the power of love.

DIVINING

In Cahuilla society, a diviner was called *tetayawis* or *tetawanis*; the term also meant "dreamer." Such a person had, among other powers, the ability to foretell future events.[39] "I had a premonition," relates Anna. "It was on Christmas a couple of years ago. . . . My daughter had a little Honda. . . . She kept saying: 'I'm gonna go now' [to their friends for Christmas dinner]. She was going to take Tracie with her. I kept saying: 'No. . . . I do not want you driving out there.' And she says: 'Oh, Mom!'" Anna insisted: "No! I've got a funny feeling. I don't want you going. You can just wait and go with us." Dean Dawn warned his daughter: "You better listen to your mother. When she [feels] something that strongly, and she keeps telling you no, . . . [then] don't do it." Her mother pleaded: "I've got a funny feeling that keeps coming. It keeps coming. It's getting stronger and stronger" (5–40, 41). Patricia nevertheless left with Tracie.

When Dean and Anna traveled to the friends' home, they did not take their normal route. "Somehow or other, I told my husband: 'Let's go down the Long Beach Freeway.' . . . I kept seeing this car. . . . It just flashed in front of my mind. It was a Honda." Shortly, they did see a Honda alongside the freeway. "Guess whose car it was?" asks Anna. "A tire had fallen off and went clear across the highway, . . . and evidently Tracie was praying so hard we'd come" (5–41). Anna repeats that normally they would have taken a different route. "But something made me make my husband go that way." When they reached Patricia's car, Anna immediately inquired if they were hurt. Patricia responded that they were not injured, then said, "Don't say it mother." But Anna could not resist. "What did I tell you? I had a feeling something was going to happen to that car" (5–42).

When asked how old she was when she had her first premonition, Anna replies that she was around eleven or twelve years old. "My mother worked at a bakery, . . . down in Watts. . . . And every Friday she'd always ask me to come down to help her so she could get through. And I always went down there, made a point not to do anything else, . . . so she could get home early. This Friday, . . . something kept telling me: 'Don't go.' . . . Well, I pushed it aside [at first]. . . . Something kept saying all day long: 'Don't go.' So when my mother called to see where I was, I says: 'Mom, I don't think I'd better come down. . . . I got a kind of funny feeling.'" Her mother pleaded with her to come to the bakery to help her so that she wouldn't have to work all night. "So I caught the bus and went down there. . . . Well, that's the night I got in an accident. The streetcar hit us, the central streetcar. I got forty stitches across my head." Because Belva had disregarded Anna's premonition, "she blamed herself for that" (6–10, 11).

This type of premonition is explained by Bean as the *tewlavilem*'s "advising, sanctioning, and aiding those still on earth."[40] Anna believes that heeding these premonitions and dreams can be beneficial. "I was dreaming that I had fell down and broke my leg. In my dream, somebody, I don't know whose voice it was, but somebody kept saying: 'Be careful, Ann. Be careful.'" She did have a near accident, slipping and twisting her ankle. "But I happened to grab a hold of the [handle on] the refrigerator, and I said: 'Oh, God, don't let me fall. . . . Don't let me get hurt.' . . . It was in my dream that I was going to fall" (17–5). She believes that because of the warning in her dream, she was able to avoid serious injury.

In the concept of power in the Luiseño world view, innate ayelkwi is the knowledge with which the individual is born. The immediate sources of innate knowledge are not entirely clear, nor are the means by which the transmission is accomplished. But it is clear that this form of knowledge is inherited.[41] When asked if anyone else in her family had these powers, Anna responds: "My grandmother and my mother. They were both that way. . . . Oh, God, yes."

She relates an incident that happened on one Friday the thirteenth. The story illustrates a blending of white superstition with Indian divining. Anna and Dean had planned a little trip, but Belva warned them not to go. "'Honey, I don't want you going . . . till after midnight. . . . I just have a funny feeling that if you go, something's going to happen.' So we didn't go. And then she told me what it was. . . . She had a vision of us getting in a wreck" (5–51). Anna emphasizes that her grandmother had the same power: "She could just . . . more or less predict that it was going to happen. And it did. . . . Or she'd sense that [someone] was very, very ill. And she'd go visit, and they were very, very ill. And she never even knew it. They never called and told her" (5–52).

Anna makes no distinction between these types of experiences, protecting loved ones and friends through divining, and those of a more materialistic nature. She used the power to help her gamble in Las Vegas, observing slot machines that seemed to point a finger at her. "I put my money in, and boy, you should have heard the screams. I hit the jackpot. . . . I don't show my emotions when I win anything. I just stand there, and everybody says: 'God! Aren't you excited? [You are] not jumping up and down and screaming.' I said: 'Now what's the sense of doing that?'" (17–16). Anna's expression of the excitement of hiting the jackpot may well be an individual character trait, or it may be a remnant of the traditional belief in moderation and personal control. The Cahuilla individual was discouraged from displaying excessive zeal.[42]

The powers of a tetayawis, a diviner, included the ability to find lost objects.[43] A combination of divining powers is revealed in the following narration by Anna. She explains, "I had a feeling that something was gonna happen to me that day, but I didn't know what it was." It turned out to be the theft of her gold Cadillac. After she discovered that the car was missing from a parking lot, she said: "I knew it. . . . I had a feeling something was gonna happen, and this is what happened." The police told her the car was probably on its way to Mexico. But Anna divined that the car was traveling northeast of Los Angeles. She told Dean that there were four black people in the car. "And they're playing my tapes" (5–55). Several weeks later, the police phoned to inform Anna that they had found her car in Las Vegas, along with the four blacks who had stolen it.

Anna frequently used her powers for a very practical purpose. She would send messages to Dean, who was a truck driver. "Dean, I forgot to tell you to get something [at the market]. Can you understand I'm trying to get through to you? . . . I want to put my thoughts in your mind. . . . Dean, please read my mind. Stop at the store and get what I'm telling you to get." When Dean arrived home, he would say: "You're pretty cute, honey. I got your message." And he would have exactly the things Anna had wanted him to get (7–9).

Either the gift of divining has not been inherited by Patricia, or she may manifest it later in her life.[44]

Pat believes that she did not inherit the power. "I think it kind of passed me over." A distinct change in the perception of supernatural power is revealed when she states: "I'm glad it did, because I don't like things like that. I don't like the feeling that something bad is gonna happen" (14–25). She finds Anna's powers "eerie, very eerie." She characterizes them as "witchcraft" (14–27). When asked if she believes that this kind of power can also be a force for good, she replies that she does but admits that she is still uncomfortable with such gifts. "It's a very eerie feeling that they can tell somebody [they] are close to that something is going to happen. You wonder what's going to happen" (14–28).

Pat does report experiences of metaphysical "sympathy pains" with her mother. She will ask Anna, "Is your shoulder bothering you?" Patricia will be feeling pain in the same spot on her shoulder. "I've had them with my daughter, too." She says that if someone she is close to has an ache, she will "pick it up." She adds: "And it hurts just as bad as if I really had it. It's weird" (14–29, 30).

Although Tracie has as yet experienced no incidents of divining, both she and Pat respect these gifts of their elders. Patricia remembers with awe when her great-grandmother, Anna May Helm, accurately divined that Tracie, when she was a young child, was going to be critically ill. Patricia also attests that the day she disregarded her mother's premonition and had an accident in the Honda was "one big turning point in [her] life" (14–26).

SUMMARY

White stresses that metaphysical beliefs, being deeply involved in the social and psychological structures of a culture, frequently show great resistance to change.[45] Despite this resistance, change does appear to be occurring in the Dawn family. Although Anna's premonition about the accident with the Honda made Patricia a "believer," and although Patricia would very much like to communicate with her deceased loved ones through a seance, there is a qualitative change in her thinking regarding the gift of divining. Patricia is relieved that she did not inherit this power, and Tracie reports only interest that her grandmother has this gift, claiming neither regret nor relief that she herself does not.

Testimony to the resilience of religion, to which White refers, is found in the remnants of metaphysical beliefs and powers possessed by this Cupeño family in Los Angeles. It is appropriate for research on American Indians to include the supernatural as well as the natural, since Indian families may contain not only elders but also spirits of elders, not only family members who care about each other but also spirits who manifest concern. Anna's good feelings that she has said goodnight to "Gram," "Mom," and "Honey" and Patricia's nightly greeting—"Hi, group, let me tell you about my day"—are evidence that in this Cupeño family, the spirits are vital participants.

CHAPTER 6

CONCLUSION

Yengine: *Cupan for "to tell the truth"*

"Man tells stories," says N. Scott Momaday, "in order to understand his experience, whatever it may be." Momaday reminds us that oral tradition is "always one generation away from extinction."[1] When asked if she believes that the Indians of Pala are aware of the precarious nature of oral tradition and of their culture, Sister Mary Yarger, former principal of Mission San Antonio de Pala School, responded that they probably are not. She articulates her belief in the persistence of tradition:

I think most of us have a tendency in the twentieth century to live in the now. . . . If we don't step forward, we're in the past. But we can't let go of the foot we still have in the past. . . . One foot is always back. When that foot steps forward, the [other] foot is in the past again. That's the only way you can . . . progress in a sequential order. . . . If we want to say: "Oh, yes, we're Indian," and someone asks: "What does that mean?" and we say that we don't know, then we're not Indian. . . . We are nothing. . . . It means we have to believe in ourselves enough to keep the past and to step forward into the future. (23–18, 19)

An awareness that Cupeño culture is one generation away from extinction is declared in an inscription near the door of the Cupa Cultural Center:

Our need is desperate. The elders of the Pala Indian Reservation are coming to the end of their years. With them is dying our rich cultural heritage. Time is of the essence to keep alive the songs, dances, art, and language of our people. We built our culture center for our people to learn and enjoy the richness of the past as part of the present. Important historical and cultural material is being lost. In order to preserve it for ourselves and make it come alive for our young people, we need financial help. Our land keeps us alive; our cultural ways make us proud to be Indian. As our elders die, so does the knowledge of the old ways. Please help us to make it possible to pass the knowledge on. Our spirit must not die.[2]

The fear regarding the death of traditional culture was expressed more than fifty years ago by a California Indian: "In the beginning, God gave to every people a cup, a cup of clay, and from this cup they drank their life. . . . Our cup is broken now."[3] The conclusion that the Cupeño cup of life is broken may easily be drawn from the facts that fewer than 150 people now claim Cupeño ethnicity, the last native speaker of Cupeño has died, and very little of precontact lifeways is apparent.[4]

The inscription in the Cupa Cultural Center continues, "In this material world, the material things which represent our heritage, the baskets, the songs, the dances, the language, can house the spirit of our culture." I suggest that another source for the spirit of this culture exists: the mentalité of individuals with Cupeño ethnicity. Moreover, although old forms of the culture may have disappeared, new forms may have been generated.

The urban Indian women in this study demonstrate a remarkable resilience and adaptability, and these characteristics create new forms of ethnicity. The principal conclusion I have drawn in this study is that, as Kenneth Lincoln suggests, Indians do redefine themselves in the city.[5] Although it sometimes appears in unexpected forms, Cupeño culture lives in modified form in the mentalité of at least one urban Indian family.

EMERGENT ETHNICITY

In a discussion of what scholars in anthropology and related fields have come to call emergent ethnicity,[6] anthropologist Michael J. Fischer states: "Ethnicity is something reinvented and reinterpreted in each generation by each individual. . . . Ethnicity is not something which is simply passed on from generation to generation. It is something dynamic."[7] Anna's interest in all things Indian is an illustration of this type of emergent ethnicity. She yearns for a tepee, a totem pole, and a Plains Indian headdress "with real eagle feathers," all of which are not indigenous to her Cupeño heritage. Nor is this expression of ethnicity something she learned from her elders. Yet her avid enthusiasm for her pan-Indian art collection, which dominates her otherwise typical middle-class house, is the spark that has ignited Tracie's desire to learn more about her Cupeño background.

Pan-Indianism illustrates the phenomenon that assuming an ethnic identity is an insistence on a pluralistic, multidimensional or multifaceted concept of self.[8] In her narrations, Anna has expressed pride in being "Mission Indian" and regret that both whites and Indians are ignorant about California American Indians. Nevertheless, the family's immersion in Indian culture is multidimensional. On one occasion, I brought glossy photos of Indian actors of various tribes to give to Anna and Pat. Both women expressed keen interest in every photo. "This one looks Indian. Look at his hair," remarked Patricia. Anna found one woman actor especially beautiful "in an Indian way." Pat did not want her mother to keep one photo because the actor did not look Indian. "He's wearing a sweater." Anna insisted that the actor did look Indian. When I asked Pat why she objected to the photo, she again complained about the sweater, saying that it was "too modern looking." Anna was full of gratitude: "I'd love to have these. I'll frame them. If you ever want them back, you'll get them framed." A few weeks later, the photos of Indians of many diverse tribes were framed and hung on the walls of Anna's living room and den. They are regarded with respect and affection by all the Dawn women, almost as though they were photos of relatives.

Anthropologist Evon Z. Vogt argues that pan-Indianism "provides a social and cultural framework within which acculturating Indian groups can maintain their sense of identity and integrity as Indians."[9] Weibel-Orlando speculates that pan-Indianism can "only be born from an urban womb" and concludes that pan-Indianism is part of the creative process by which an urban Indian community defines itself.[10] The pan-Indianism of the Dawns supports both these arguments.

In their perceptions of their relationships with "all their relatives," the Dawns manifest the strongest ties to tribal traditions. Even in this area, though, changes in their mentalité reveal emergent forms of ethnicity. The importance of the elders in Indian families, stressed by a number of scholars, has not been diminished in the urban Dawn family. Anna and Patricia made conscious decisions to raise their children as closely as possible to the manner in which they themselves were brought up, and

Tracie plans to have her mother and her grandmother help raise her children. Each woman believes that she has been taught by her mother and her grandmother the values necessary for a successful and happy life.

There is, nevertheless, an apparent change in Pat's attitude toward discipline. She articulates and often manifests the same attitude as her mother about strict obedience, but when confronted with a Madonna "wanna-be," Patricia decided to ignore the problem and wait for Tracie to start "growing up." Although Tracie clearly loves and respects her mother and her grandmother, her obedience to them was diminished, at least temporarily, by her attraction to an icon of white youth, the rock singer Madonna.

Tradition shows considerable persistence in the close interrelationships of the Dawn family members. New forms of ethnicity, all powered by love, have emerged out of the complexities created by divorce. Patricia had "Dad One" and "Dad Two" give her away at her wedding; Anna, Patricia, and Anna's ex-husband's wife, Betty, enjoy each other "like three kids"; and Tracie loves her stepsiblings, whom she refuses to characterize as "step." These are only a few illustrations of the enduring and versatile interrelatedness in this remarkable family.

Their belief in being "related everywhere," as the Cahuilla say, emerged in my relationship with the Dawn women. Having invited my husband and me to celebrate my birthday with them, each woman independently told him, "Because Diana is our family, you are, too." The evening ended with a moving, almost formulaic pronouncement by Anna, "As my daughter has said, as my granddaughter has said, I say: 'You are family.'"

A change in my own mentalité, a heightened sensitivity to people in need, emerged from my listening to the Dawn narrations of beneficence. Although the Dawns are most likely following tradition in their generosity, the urban mutations of this beneficence can be neither ignored nor completely explained. In its spontaneous, direct, and personalized form, their generosity appears to adhere to tribal patterns. In its abstraction of reciprocity and community benefit, their beneficence is, indeed, a form of ethnicity that has emerged in an urban milieu.

John Red Horse, specialist in research on American Indian families, refers to the phenomenon of mistaking different patterns for an erosion of Indian cultural values, arguing that core values are retained and remain as a constant.[11] An illustration of a core value persisting in altered form is found in the gifts placed on the graves of the Indian cemetery in Pala. The Catholic priest at Pala can understand the expected and traditional gift of an eagle feather, but a man's boots? The priest seems bewildered by this changed form in which Indian spirituality is expressed.

When I began this study, I expected to find some forms of traditional beliefs in the mentalité of the Dawn women, but I was not prepared for the extent to which their metaphysical experiences reflect the literature on patterns of spirituality. The integration of the natural and the supernatural, especially in communications with the dead, persists in the Dawn family. Because of the strength of past and present relationships in this family, all three women have no fear of the spirits of their deceased loved ones. Indeed, they appear to be comforted by these spirits.

The core value of the belief in supernatural power is retained, although the power is manifested in changing forms. Conducting seances and making the table move represent a relatively new form of accessing power. Anna traces it back only to her grandmother's generation. Anna's gift for divining is manifested in several forms that have emerged from an urban life-style: assisting her in hitting the jackpot on slot machines in Las Vegas; providing her with information regarding the theft of her car, information to which even the police did not have access; and enabling her to send thought messages to her husband to get things she needed at the market. Although Patricia believes she has not inherited her mother's powers, the "sympathy pains" she experiences are either her reinterpretation of this type of power or another manifestation of the power that is generated by the close relationships in this family.

Will the ethnicity continue to persist, either in traditional or emergent forms? Ethnicity will endure through the telling of the Dawn family's stories. The strongest evidence for this conclusion is found in the family members' narrations. The need to tell about their Indianness, evident from the beginning, became stronger as the interviews proceeded. The concept of cultural survival through oral tradition has a long history with American Indians and is a recurring theme in Indian literature.

Simon Ortiz, Acoma Pueblo, expresses the belief in survival through oral tradition in his poem "Survival This Way." The poem reads in part: "We travelled this way, gauged our distance by stories. . . . We told ourselves over and over again, 'We shall survive this way.'"[12] Believing that memory and imagination are not always easily distinguished, Leslie Marmon Silko, of Laguna Pueblo, states, "As with any generation, the oral tradition depends upon each person listening and remembering a portion, and it is together—all of us remembering what we have heard together—that creates the whole story, the long story of the people."[13] Anna, Patricia, and Tracie, by listening and remembering, have encoded what they consider to be vital about their family, thus creating their part of the Cupeño story that is still being told.

Geertz believes that the achievement of "thick description," or generality, emerges from "the delicacy of its distinction, not the sweep of its abstractions."[14] This study, focusing on identifying distinctions through changes in mentalité, discovers that although Anna, Patricia, and Tracie all perceive a Cupeño identity, each reveals her own unique interpretation of this ethnicity.

Ronald Cohen, scholar in anthropology and political science, states, "Persons are not roles."[15] Yet I suggest that role does play a vital part in the individual's perception of ethnicity. Pat and Tracie, at this point in their lives, may defer to Anna as the keeper of their Indian heritage, just as Anna deferred to her elders earlier in life. Anna grieves over the fact that she did not heed her grandfather's warnings that she would come to regret not letting him teach her Cupeño, the tribal language. But she was young, there was time, and her grandfather protected the heritage. She perceives her role as having changed as she grew older. "It's a beautiful language. . . . It would make me real proud if I could just talk it. . . . I'd probably know it if I hadn't been so hardheaded. . . . Now, I did go to the library . . . but the only thing I could get was Navajo" (2–10).

Because of the interest in their Cupeño background expressed in their narrations, it is reasonable to assume that Patricia and Tracie may one day become keepers of their heritage. Virtually assured is the continuation of the strength of the family ties. Redhorse urges that research on American Indians should "shift from questions investigating family pathology to questions investigating family survival." Moreover, the American Indian family should be defined according to its current structure, traditional or not.[16]

One of the most disturbing findings in the literature is the discovery, noted in chapter 2, that some California Indian women suffer from a belief that they need to hide their Indian identity.[17] Since this deception is never present in the Dawn narrations, it is important to determine how the Dawns' family histories differ from those of Indians who wish to get lost in the city. L. L. Langness, Professor of Psychiatry and Anthropology at UCLA, notes, "It is in the context of the family that the interrelationships between culture and individual . . . can best be seen."[18] I assume that the family structure of the Dawns provides defenses against the alienating factors in the city, defenses not provided by the families of those who attempt to hide their Indianness. The narrations of the Dawns substantiate the work of Redhorse and others who recognize the family as the cornerstone of American Indian society.[19]

Clifford argues, "Ethnographers can no longer know the whole truth, or even claim to approach it." Nevertheless, he suggests a viable stance for the ethnographer when he quotes a Cree hunter called to testify in court. When administered the oath, the Cree hesitated: "I'm not sure I can tell the truth. . . . I can only tell what I know."[20] Anna, Patricia, and Tracie, by telling only what they know of Cupeño values and beliefs, have presented us with a significant gift.

Articulating their gift required a methodology that was inductive. In life-history research, the dynamic between the narrations and the interpretation, between the consciousness of the narrators and that of the researcher, is intrinsically emergent.[21] A similar collaborative, unfolding process is suggested by the world view of the Cupeño. Like the Quiché Maya of Guatemala among others, the Cupeño include twin creator gods in their cosmology; the culture does not trace the origin of the world to a single creator.[22] Regarding the dual creators of the world, the Quiché say: "There were always already two of them; there was no beginning from one. . . . They talked."[23] In this study of an urban Cupeño family, there was also no beginning from one. There were Anna and I, Patricia and I, Tracie and I. We talked.

AFTERWORD

As one drives along Santa Fe Avenue and adjacent streets at the time of this writing, there are haunting reminders of the violence in south-central Los Angeles following the verdict in the Rodney King trial on April 29, 1992. Within the areas immediately surrounding the Dawn home are charred remains of a number of businesses, including furniture stores, liquor stores, and worst of all, the supermarket. On Saturdays Patricia now drives to Downey, a distance of more than ten miles, to obtain necessary food items for Anna, who is diabetic.

Although the impact on the American Indian community in Los Angeles was not depicted by the non-Indian media, the *Lakota Times* reported that the Southern California Indian Center was flooded with requests for assistance, especially for baby formula, during and immediately after the riots. The center has also been providing treatment for posttraumatic syndrome for staff and residents.[1]

Considering their proximity to the riot-torn areas, the Dawn family members suffered relatively little. However, there were three days of intense concern that the fires in the riot areas, including some within a distance of two blocks, would ignite their home. Anna was kept busy retrieving burning shingles that had blown into her yard. Both Anna and Patricia tell stories about scolding people they observed looting businesses in Huntington Park. As one teenager yelled to them: "Come and get it! It's free!" Anna responded: "Put that back. It is *not* free. You should be ashamed of yourself!" Patricia was furious when she saw a young boy looting a nearby store at eleven o'clock at night. "What are you doing out here this time of night? Get your butt home!"

Despite the relative quiet since the riots, the Dawns feel that the calm may be temporary. Patricia, who learned how to handle firearms with her first husband, is prepared to arm herself. She matter-of-factly states that she is prepared to use a gun to defend her home and family, if need be.

In spite of continued tension in the city, John Castillo, director of the Southern California Indian Center, says, "The Indian community is rebounding." He attributes the resilience to moral and financial support from other Indian communities, notably San Diego and Phoenix.[2] Characteristic of her own resilience, Anna has decided to have major remodeling done on her home. Moreover, she is especially looking forward in 1992 to a civic contribution she has been making for more than twenty years: volunteer work in local polling places for the primary and general elections. She agrees with Castillo that the one good thing that has emerged from the riots is a greater sense of the importance of citizens working together.

NOTES

CHAPTER 1: INTRODUCTION

1. Bean and Smith, "Cupeño," 589.
2. To protect their privacy, I have changed the names of all living interviewees. In considering the names they wanted to use, Anna and Patricia fantasized about Indian names like Evening Star and Morning Dove but ultimately selected more modest pseudonyms. The selection did not take place, however, without some teasing. Recalling an incident in which Anna had purchased at a powwow a "genuine" buffalo-bone necklace, which turned her neck and blouse black, Pat suggested "Little Black Neck" as the name for her mother.
3. Frank, "Finding the Common Denominator," 70.
4. Titon, "The Life Story," 281.
5. See Shaw's "Life History Writing an Anthropology" for a survey of life-history scholarship.
6. Hertzberg, *An American Indian Identity*, viii.
7. Hanson, "The Urban Indian Woman," 478.
8. Green states that her review of more than seven hundred bibliographic items on native North American women left her with the conviction that despite great interest in these women, they have been presented in "selective, stereotyped, and damaging" portrayals (*Native American Women*, 1).
9. The numbers refer to the tape transcript and page. For example, 1–9 refers to tape transcript number 1, page 9. The transcripts are in the possession of the author. Copies of the tapes and transcripts are also archived at Southwest Museum, Los Angeles.
10. A useful discussion of categories of American Indian identity is found in Snipp, "On the Costs of Being an American Indian," 424–26.
11. Hertzberg, *An American Indian Identity*, vii.

12. Moses and Wilson, "Introduction," *Indian Lives*, 4–5.

13. Ibid., 7.

14. Berkhofer, *The White Man's Indian*, xv.

15. Stedman, *Shadows of the Indian*, x.

16. Berkhofer, *The White Man's Indian*, 25–26.

17. A seminal study of the pressure on Indians to assimilate is Pearce's *Savagism and Civilization*.

18. Bataille and Silet, "Introduction," *The Pretend Indians*, xxviii.

19. Hanson and Rouse, "Dimensions of Native American Stereotyping."

20. Snipp, "On the Costs of Being an American Indian"; Simmons, "One Little, Two Little, Three Little Indians."

21. Cook, "Historical Demography," 93.

22. Field notes.

23. It is important to make a distinction between actual blood quantum, which is often very difficult to determine, and mentalité regarding blood. In Anna's mentalité, she is a full-blood American Indian, Cupeño on her mother's side and Apache on her father's, although the latter cannot be documented by the family. Consequently, Patricia and Tracie also perceive Anna as being full-blood and see themselves as half and one-quarter Indians, respectively.

24. Momaday, *The Names*, 25.

25. Lincoln, *Native American Renaissance*, 185.

26. John Castillo, director of the Southern California Indian Center, telephone conversation, February 26, 1992. For a discussion of the problems encountered in administering the census to American Indian populations, see Slagle, "Review Article."

27. Lincoln, *Native American Renaissance*, 185, 187.

28. Tax, "The Impact of Urbanization," 135; Edmunds in Trafzer, *American Indian Identity*, 1–6.

29. Longfish, "Contemporary Native American Art."

30. Hertzberg, *An American Indian Identity*; Lurie, "The Enduring Indian"; Pearce, *Savagism and Civilization*; Price, "Migration and Adaptation"; Stewart, "Urbanization, Peoplehood, and Modes of Identity."

31. Price, "The Migration and Adaptation of American Indians to Los Angeles."

32. An informative discussion of historical pan-Indian movements is presented in Hertzberg, *An American Indian Identity*.

33. Price, "The Migration and Adaptation of American Indians to Los Angeles."

34. Momaday, "The Man Made of Words," 97.

35. Field notes.

36. Several scholars, notably Green, *Native American Women*, and Albers and Medicine, *The Hidden Half*, have noted the paucity of realistic portrayals of individual American Indian women, especially in a modern context.

37. Clifford, "Partial Truths," 26.

38. Langness and Frank, *Lives*; Shaw, "Life History Writing"; Robinson, "Personal Narratives Reconsidered."

39. Frank, "Finding the Common Denominator," 72. Duby also argues that behavior is shaped not by a "real condition" but by people's inaccurate perception of that condition ("Ideologies in Social History," 151). Similarly, Geertz believes that descriptions of other cultures are interpretations of interpretations, resulting in a lack of precise criteria for life history ("Thick Description," 15).

40. LeGoff and Nora, *Constructing the Past*, 170.

41. Bean, *Mukat's People*, 15.

42. McFee finds an urban Indian population segment that is highly bicultural, moving with ease within white culture while still being Indian-oriented. Ablon speaks of a similar group that is pan-Indian in orientation, a functional alternative to tribal identity in the city. The same phenomenon is described by Wax as the "generalized" Indian, one who maintains multiple cultural identities in the city. For a review of this scholarship see Stewart, "Urbanization, Peoplehood, and Modes of Identity."

43. Wagner's study of Indian women in New York City concluded that a white husband is a "potent maximizing agent" in the acculturation of urban Indian women and that intermarried Indian women are more inclined to remain in the city ("An Examination and Description of Acculturation," 221).

44. Stewart, "Urbanization, Peoplehood, and Modes of Identity," 128–29. Stewart's model emphasizes behavioral change, a focus that has shifted in more recent emphases on ideational aspects of culture. Culture-change models that consider only behavior neglect mentalité, which can persist even after the behavioral manifestations no longer exist.

45. Allen, "Who Is Your Mother?," 13–14.

46. Geertz, "The Struggle for the Real," 111–12.

CHAPTER 2: HISTORICAL CONTEXT

1. This biographical account is a compilation of field notes and information in *San Diego County Pioneer Fami-*

lies: *A Collection of Family Histories Compiled by the San Diego Historical Society*, 1977 (P.O. Box 81825, San Diego, CA 92138). When referring to their grandparents, Anna, Patricia, and Tracie reveal a congruence in mentalité. Unless specifically asked for clarification, they never refer to them as "great-" or "great-great-."

2. Bahr, "An End To Invisibility," 409.

3. Jackson and Kinney, *The Mission Indians of California*, 458.

4. Shipek, "History of Southern California Mission Indians," 610.

5. Shipek provides a concise and informative discussion of the missionization of California Indians in *Pushed into the Rocks*, 19–24.

6. Costo and Henry, *The Missions of California*.

7. An excellent discussion of the Black Legend and the White Legend is presented by Rawls, *Indians in California*, 34–43. The Black Legend has been bolstered by the recent scholarship of Carrico, "American Indian Self-Determination"; Castillo, "Euro-American Exploration"; Forbes, "American Indian Experience"; Shipek, *Pushed into the Rocks*; Thornton, *American Indian Holocaust*, who describe the California mission system as totalitarian and coercive. Lothrop, however, presents an argument for an evaluation of Serra within "an honest and informed appraisal of his era" ("El Viejo: Serra in Context," 16).

8. Thornton, *American Indian Holocaust*, 109; Cook, "Historical Demography," 91.

9. Cook, "Historical Demography," 91.

10. Consult the works of Carrico, "American Indian Self-Determination"; Cook, *The Conflict Between the Indian and White Civilization*; Forbes, "American Indian Experience"; Rawls, *Indians in California*; Shipek, *Pushed into the Rocks*; and Thornton, *American Indian Holocaust*.

11. Cook, *The Conflict between the California Indian and White Civilization*.

12. Shipek, *Pushed into the Rocks*, 23–24.

13. Coffer, "Genocide of the California Indians," 11.

14. Phillips, *Chiefs and Challengers*, 181 n. 41.

15. Bean and Smith, "Cupeño," 590.

16. Lummis, "The Exiles of Cupa."

17. Bean and Smith, "Cupeño"; Bright and Hill, "The Linguistic History of the Cupeño"; Shipek, *Pushed into the Rocks*.

18. Bean and Smith, "Cupeño," 588; Alfred Kroeber, *Handbook of the Indians of California*, 689.

19. Quoted in Hill and Nolasquez, *Mulu'Wetam*, 49a, no. X.

20. Ibid., 1.

21. Alfred Kroeber, *Handbook of the Indians of California*, 690.

22. Bean and Smith, "Cupeño"; Hill and Nolasquez, *Mulu'Wetam*; Alfred Kroeber, *Handbook of the Indians of California*; Phillips, *Chiefs and Challengers*; Strong, *Aboriginal Society*.

23. Hill and Nolasquez, *Mulu'Wetam*, 1.

24. Heizer, "Natural Forces," 649.

25. Strong, *Aboriginal Society*, 190.

26. Kroeber and Heizer, *Almost Ancestors*, and Bean and Smith, "Cupeño."

27. Bean, *Mukat's People*, 161, 173; Bean, "Cahuilla," 581.

28. Heizer, "Natural Forces and Native World View"; Alfred Kroeber, *Handbook of the Indians of California*; Bean and Shipek, "Luiseño."

29. Kroeber, *Handbook of the Indians of California*, 683.

30. Bean and Smith, "Cupeño"; Castillo, "Euro-American Exploration"; Hill and Nolasquez, *Mulu'Wetam*; Jackson, "Report on the Conditions and Needs of the Mission Indians"; Strong, *Aboriginal Society*.

31. Hill and Nolasquez, *Mulu'Wetam*, 1.

32. Bean and Smith, "Cupeño," 589.

33. Hill and Nolasquez, *Mulu'Wetam*, 1; Strong, *Aboriginal Society*, 184.

34. Hill and Nolasquez, *Mulu'Wetam*, 1.

35. Lummis, "The Exiles of Cupa," 471.

36. Castillo, "Euro-American Exploration," 108, 114.

37. Jackson and Kinney, *The Mission Indians of California*, 463–64.

38. For a complete history of the Garra uprising, see Phillips, *Chiefs and Challengers*, 175.

39. Castillo, "Euro-American Exploration," 114.

40. Jackson and Kinney, *The Mission Indians of California*, 486.

41. Ibid.

42. Hill and Nolasquez, *Mulu'Wetam*, 92–96; Lummis, "The Exiles of Cupa"; and Wallace, "The Exiles of Cupa."

43. Lummis, "The Exiles of Cupa," 465.

44. Lummis, "Turning a New Leaf," 442–43.

45. Ibid., 444.

46. Ibid., 445, 449.

47. Hill and Nolasquez, *Mulu'Wetam*, 96 n. 66.

48. Kelsey, "Report of Special Agent for California Indians," 143.

49. Lummis, "Turning a New Leaf," 446.

50. Lummis, "The Exiles of Cupa," 470.

51. Ibid., 475.

52. Wallace, "The Exiles of Cupa," 31.

53. Ibid., 37.

54. Hill and Nolasquez, *Mulu'Wetam*, 23a, no. IX.

55. Ibid., 21a, no. VIII.

56. Ibid., 22a.

57. Wallace, "The Exiles of Cupa," 39–41.

58. Hill and Nolasquez tell, in Cupeño oral history, how the natives had originally built homes with tule and grass before the "bald people" taught them how to build adobe houses (*Mulu'Wetam*, 50a, no. XII).

59. Kelsey, "Report of Special Agent for California Indians," 144.

60. Field notes.

61. Ibid.

62. Carrico, "American Indian Self-Determination," 199.

63. Blackburn, "Ceremonial Integration," 229.

64. Hill and Nolasquez, *Mulu'Wetam*, 154.

65. Field notes.

66. Carrico, "American Indian Self-Determination," 199.

67. Cook, *The Population of the California Indians*, 176.

68. Beale, "Migration Patterns of Minorities in the United States," 944.

69. Bean and Smith, "Cupeño," 589.

70. Cook, "Migration and Urbanization of Indians in California," 557.

71. Cook, "Historical Demography," 98.

72. Bahr, "An End to Invisibility," 404–9.

73. The prohibition of the sale of liquor to Indians was stopped in 1953 as part of the campaign to repeal federal legislation that set Indians apart from other citizens. For discussions of the long history of federal prohibition of the sale of liquor to Indians, see Hoxie, *A Final Promise*, 221–30, and Prucha, *The Great Father*, 8–9, 40–41, 106–7, 115, 270–71, 347.

74. Bahr, Chadwick, and Day, *Native Americans Today*, 401.

75. Simross, "The Plight of Native Americans," 1.

76. Larsen, "The Invisible Minority," 1.

77. Thornton, Sandefur, and Grasmick, *The Urbanization of American Indians*, 19. Price, "Migration and Adaptation," concludes that Indians move to Los Angeles for better jobs, wages, and living conditions. His findings are similar to those of Graves, "Drinking and Drunkenness," Sorkin, *The Urban Indian*, and Guillemin, *Urban Rene-*

gades, all of whom identify economics as the major motivation for relocation in the city.

78. Thornton, Sandefur, and Grasmick, "The Urbanization of American Indians, 27.

79. *Ethnic Groups in Los Angeles*, 16. Indians in Los Angeles have a lower poverty rate than blacks in Los Angeles (28 percent of females and 24 percent of males) and than Hispanics (25.6 percent of females and 22.9 percent of males). Nevertheless, the percentage of American Indians in Los Angeles living in households with an annual income below the federal threshold of $13,359 is considerably higher than the 13.5 percent of the total population nationally who are reported as living below this poverty line.

80. For discussions of rural-urban migrations of American Indians, see Graves, "Drinking and Drunkenness"; Sorkin, *The Urban Indian*; Guillemin, *Urban Renegades*; Jorgensen, "Indians and the Metropolis"; Price, "Migration and Adaptation"; Stauss and Chadwick, "Urban Indian Adjustment."

81. Price, "Migration and Adaptation," concludes that long-term participation in the Indian "bar culture" of Los Angeles is dysfunctional. Fiske argues that this behavior is not dysfunctional for all Indians ("Urban Institutions," 167 n.5). Guillemin believes that public drinking and fighting is a "risk-taking venture" that explores the boundaries of appropriate behavior for Indian men in the city (*Urban Renegades*, 10). Weibel-Orlando cites evidence that the Indian bar is being replaced by other social institutions. Her studies substantiate other scholars' findings that American Indians who migrated to the city during the past fifty years found the move alienating and stressful. She concludes that the consequent "cultural overload" may lead to social marginality, an underlying cause of alcoholism (*Indian Country, L.A.*, 242–45).

82. Among the prevalent health problems of older Indians in Los Angeles, sadness and grieving were reported in 1989 by 22.4 percent (Weibel-Orlando, *Urban American Indian Elders Outreach Project*, 113).

83. Sorkin finds American Indians living in the "most blighted" areas of the city (*The Urban Indian*, 83). Stauss and Chadwick report that 70 percent of the Seattle Indians in their sample had experienced housing discrimination ("Urban Indian Adjustment," 33). Beale finds that unlike other minority migrants, Indians move directly to an urban fringe, intermediate between the inner city and the affluent white areas ("Migration Patterns of Minorities," 944).

84. Larsen, "The Invisible Minority," 1.

85. Cohen, "Ethnicity," 401.

86. Wiebel, "Native Americans in Los Angeles," 359–60.

87. Guillemin, *Urban Renegades*, 10.

88. Thornton, Sandefur, and Grasmick, *The Urbanization of American Indians*, 32. For the most recent research on American Indian families, see Red Horse, Lewis, Felt, Decker, "American Indian Elders," and Hanson, "The Urban Indian Woman."

89. Native American Research Group, *Native American Socialization*, 20.

90. Ibid., 22.

CHAPTER 3: PERCEPTIONS OF FAMILY AND INDIVIDUALITY

1. Field notes.

2. Ryan, "Strengths of the American Indian Family," 25, 30.

3. Miller, "Alternative Paradigms," 84.

4. This claim regarding the significance of the family's influence is consistently reiterated by all three women. No counterevidence emerged in the narrations. The full extent of the intensity and the scope of various influences in these life histories can be determined only by a study that goes beyond the mentalité of the narrators.

5. Field notes.

6. Ibid.

7. Hammer, *Daughters and Mothers*, xiv. For literature on intergenerational relationships among women, see also Kornhaber and Woodward, *Grandparents, Grandchildren*, and Adams, *Kinship*.

8. Bean, *Mukat's People*, 174–75.

9. Field notes.

10. Neisser, *Mothers and Daughters*; Freeman, *Who Is Sylvia?*; Friday, *My Mother/Myself*; and Hammer, *Daughters and Mothers*, all discuss the issue of "the separate self." This issue emerges as a salient theme in studies of multigenerational families. Cohler and Grunebaum discovered that bonds based on interdependency could lead to conflict as well as cohesion (*Mothers, Grandmothers, and Daughters*, 315). They also conclude, however, that because of a bias toward the value of independence,

"family theory has had great difficulty dealing with the fact of continuing closeness." They argue that continuing interaction in a multigenerational family "provides an important source of ego strength, identity and sense of personal congruence" (ibid., 332).

11. Bean and Shipek, "Luiseño," 555.

12. A comparison is found in the study of families in the Oakland area, *Native American Socialization to Urban Life*, 50. The data show that 50 percent of California Indians administered discipline to children who stayed away from home without permission. Only the Sioux reported a higher percentage, 53 percent.

13. Of all the tribes surveyed in the Oakland study, California Indians reported the highest percentage, 63 percent, of families who discipline children for talking back to parents (*Native American Socialization to Urban Life*, 50).

14. In 1822, Father Jeronimo Boscana wrote: "So great is the affection which they have for their dances that they will spend days, nights, and whole weeks dancing. . . . All their passion is given to dancing, for few days pass that they do not have a dance. . . . They were of the belief that those who did not dance . . . and those who did not attend dances were to be punished and hated by their God Chinigchinix" (Harrington, *A New Original Version*, 38).

15. Alfred Kroeber, *Handbook of the Indians of California*, 683; Bean and Shipek, "Luiseño," 556.

16. Advice to adolescents during puberty rites stressed being cordial to relatives-in-law (Alfred Kroeber, *Handbook of the Indians of California*, 683; Heizer, "Natural Forces," 652; Bean and Shipek, "Luiseño," 556.

17. Harvey, "The Luiseño," 162.

18. Bean and Shipek, "Luiseño," 552.

19. Weibel-Orlando quoted in Larsen, "The Invisible Minority," 12. Red Horse argues, however, that although both the nuclear and the extended family models can be found in American Indian family systems, these models are not limiting parameters ("Family Structure," 462–63).

20. Bean, *Mukat's People*, 91.

21. Bean observes that even a spouse's death did not destroy the integrity of Cahuilla families ("Cahuilla," 581).

22. In Cahuilla tradition, "failure to reciprocate was a serious breach of behavioral norms. Integrity and dependability in personal relations were sought constantly. . . . Actions were expected to be as explicit and direct as possible in order to reduce misunderstandings" (ibid., 583).

23. Red Horse, "American Indian Families," 1–2; Miller, "Paradigms for Available Research," 82.

24. Tracie's accounts of the Dawn life history dramatize the assertions of Red Horse, who says, "Interdependence leads elders not into retirement, but into vital affairs of the family" (*American Indian Family*, 2). Red Horse goes so far as to argue: "Indian survival requires the recognition . . . of traditional family structure and discipline—a discipline designed around relationships, respect, and extraordinary commitment to each other" ("Family Structure," 492).

CHAPTER 4: BENEFICENCE

1. Clifford, "Partial Truths," 18.

2. Geertz, *Local Knowledge*, 70.

3. Weibel, "Native Americans in Los Angeles," 360.

4. Forbes, "The Native American Experience in California History," 236.

5. Personal correspondence, May 7, 1990.

6. Discussing the concept of power in native California, Bean states, "In order to acquire power, one must behave honestly, prudently, moderately and reciprocally in relation to others" ("Power and its Applications," 412). Bean also argues that generosity is a euphemism for reciprocity and that its adaptive function is clear: it provides "a compensatory mechanism to cope with real or felt imbalances . . . in the economic and social system" (*Mukat's People*, 174–75).

7. Tax declares, "Native Americans are among the few peoples who maintain kinship and sharing cultures which contrast greatly with our large, economically oriented, individualized, impersonal, urbanizing society." Tax explains this phenomenon. "Indian people from time immemorial have explored and found ways to live in new environments without losing their identities or values" ("The Impact of Urbanization," 121, 134). In her study of Indians in Los Angeles, Fiske concludes, "There is no disputing the fact that friendship and kinship networks are very important institutions in the Indian community." She concurs with Weibel in believing that most Indians prefer to rely on other Indians for help ("Urban Institutions," 157, 162).

8. Zunz, *The Changing Face of Inequality*, 61.

9. Guillemin, noting that the dominant population is "sequestered away from the poor," finds the urban Indi-

ans of her study "another group among a host of minority and poor people" (*Urban Renegades*, 13, 19).

10. Zunz, *The Changing Face of Inequality*, 261; Chudacoff, *American Urban Society*, 121.

11. Bean, *Mukat's People*, 173.

12. White, "The Luiseño Theory of Knowledge," 4. Weibel found a similar continuity of culture among Indians in Los Angeles who, even after urbanization, "are who their mothers taught them to be" ("Native Americans in Los Angeles," 360).

13. Henretta, "The Study of Social Mobility," 178.

14. Bean, *Mukat's People*, 174.

15. Price, "Migration and Adaptation," argues that overtime conditions in the city lead the American Indian away from tribal patterns, primarily because of social anonymity and the fact that the range of possible choices is increased in the city.

16. Lee, *Freedom and Culture*, argues that cooperation and harmony pervade the structure of culture and that self-fulfillment finds its fullest scope in helping and sharing. Kroeber, *Ishi in Two Worlds*, observed this manner of self-fulfillment by Ishi, the lone survivor of the Yahi tribe of California Indians, noting that nothing made him happier than to be able to give something.

CHAPTER 5: THE METAPHYSICAL REALM

1. Hultkrantz, *The Religions of the American Indians*, 10. Hultkrantz's work includes a substantive discussion of the natural and the supernatural in American Indian thought.

2. Margolin, *The Way We Lived*, 113; Forbes, "The Native American Experience in California History," 237.

3. Hultkrantz, *The Religions of the American Indians*, 1.

4. Harrington, *A New Original Version*, 10, 51, 52.

5. Powers, *Tribes of California*, 413.

6. Hultkrantz, *The Religions of the American Indians*, 19, 21.

7. Talamantez, "Use of Dialogue," 35; Alfred Kroeber, *Handbook of the Indians of California*, 691, 707, 851; Bean and Vane, "Cults and Their Transformations," 667. Despite the fact that the toloache cult is apparently very old and common to the peoples of southern California, scholars find that a precise delineation of the use of the

plant is difficult, since societies that used it had been transformed by contact with whites by the time ethnographers investigated them.

8. Bean and Vane, "Cults and Their Transformations," 669.

9. Harrington, *A New Original Version*, 2.

10. Harrington, "Fieldwork among the Indians of California," 88.

11. Harrington, *A New Original Version*, 5.

12. White, "Religion and its Rule among the Luiseño," 357.

13. Although no one in the family knows where Anna May Helm got the cloth, Professor Charlotte Heth of UCLA believes that it was most likely an Oral Roberts prayer cloth.

14. White, "Religion and its Role among the Luiseño," 367; Bean, "Power and its Applications," 413.

15. Field notes.

16. Bean, "Power and its Applications," 414.

17. Ibid., 416.

18. Bean, *Mukat's People*, 169.

19. Alfred Kroeber, *Handbook of the Indians of California*, 675.

20. Hultkrantz, *The Religions of the American Indians*, 130.

21. Underhill, "Religion among American Indians," 129.

22. Bean, *Mukat's People*, 169.

23. White, "Two Surviving Luiseño Indian Ceremonies," 569.

24. Bean, *Mukat's People*, 168–69.

25. White, "Luiseño Theory of Knowledge," 7.

26. Harrington, *A New Original Version*, 55.

27. *The Autobiography of Delfina Cuero*, 43, 44.

28. Anthropologist Paul L. Faye noted in 1928, "Acceleration in social transformations has been promoted by the forcible way in which they were wrenched from their former habitat" ("Christmas Fiestas of the Cupeño," 658).

29. Cook states: "Recognizing that some form of native ritualistic expression must be allowed, the priests more or less deliberately adopted a twofold policy . . . to redirect the instincts into what to them were proper channels, [and] they permitted the neophytes to retain a great deal of the native ceremonial insofar as the latter did not conflict with Christian morals and propriety" (*The Conflict between the California Indian and White Civilization*, 151, 153). See also Bean and Vane, "Cults and Their Transformations," 669–70.

30. Du Bois, "A Diegeño Fiesta at Mesa Grande," 56–58.

31. An article on the priest, Father John Hascall of Sacred Heart Catholic Church, appeared in the *Los Angeles Times*, February 16, 1987.

32. Field notes. See also Bean and Shipek, "Luiseño," 561.

33. Field notes.

34. Dart, "American Indians Becoming More Open to Christian Worship Services," 1, 5.

35. White, "Luiseño Theory of Knowledge," 3; Bean and Blackburn, *Native Californians*, 414.

36. Bean, *Mukat's People*, 170.

37. Ibid., 169.

38. *The Autobiography of Delfina Cuero*, 51.

39. Bean, "Cahuilla," 581.

40. Bean, *Mukat's People*, 169.

41. White, "Luiseño Theory of Knowledge," 5.

42. Bean, *Mukat's People*, 178.

43. Bean, "Cahuilla," 581.

44. The Luiseño have an explanation for differential power: a mythical ancestor threw away all of his knowledge, leaving to his descendants whatever each individually was able to recover (White, "Two Surviving Luiseño Ceremonies," 577).

45. White, "Religion and its Role among the Luiseño," 355.

CHAPTER 6: CONCLUSION

1. Momaday, "The Man Made of Words," 104, 108.

2. Field notes.

3. Benedict, *Patterns of Culture*, 19.

4. Field notes; Bean and Smith, "Cupeno," 589–90.

5. Lincoln, *Native American Renaissance*, 184–85.

6. A review of the literature on emergent ethnicity is found in Yancey, Ericksen, and Juliani, "Emergent Ethnicity."

7. Fischer, "Ethnicity," 195.

8. Ibid., 196.

9. Vogt, "The Acculturation of American Indians," 146.

10. Wiebel-Orlando, *Indian Country, L.A.*, 60.

11. Red Horse, Lewis, Felt, and Decker, "Urban American Indians," 70.

12. Ortiz, "Survival This Way," 28.

13. Silko, *Storyteller*, 6, 7.

14. Shankman, "The Thick and the Thin," 262.

15. Cohen, "Ethnicity," 401.

16. Red Horse, "American Indian Families," 7; Miller, "Alternative Paradigms," 83.

17. Native American Research Group, *Native American Socialization*, 20.

18. Langness and Frank, *Lives*, 7.

19. Red Horse, "Family Structure," 462.

20. Clifford, "Partial Truths," 8, 25.

21. Kelley calls this dynamic "an ongoing interplay between the raw data and the interpretative framework" (*Yaqui Women*, 31).

22. Bean and Smith, "Cupeño," 589.

23. Tedlock, *The Spoken Word*, 258.

AFTERWORD

1. Anquoe, "L.A. Riots," A2.

2. Ibid.

BIBLIOGRAPHY

Adams, Bert N. *Kinship in an Urban Setting*. Chicago: Markham Publishing Co., 1968.

Albers, Patricia, and Beatrice Medicine. *The Hidden Half: Studies of Plains Indian Women*. Washington, D.C.: University Press of America, 1983.

Allen, Paula Gunn. "Who Is Your Mother?" In *The Graywolf Annual Five: Multi-Cultural Literacy*, ed. Rick Simonson and Scott Walker, 13–14. Saint Paul: Graywolf Press, 1988.

Anquoe, Bunty. "L.A. Riots Shake Indian Community." *Lakota Times*, May 20, 1992, A2.

Bahr, Howard M. "An End to Invisibility," 404–9. In *Native Americans Today: Sociological Perspectives*, ed. Howard M. Bahr, Bruce A. Chadwick, and Robert C. Day. New York: Harper and Row, 1972.

Bahr, Howard M., Bruce A. Chadwick, and Robert C. Day, eds. *Native Americans Today: Sociological Perspectives*. New York: Harper and Row, 1972.

Barron, Hal S. *Those Who Stayed Behind: Rural Society in Nineteenth Century New England*. Cambridge: Cambridge University Press, 1984.

Basso, Keith. *Portraits of "The Whiteman."* Cambridge: Cambridge University Press, 1979.

Bataille, Gretchen, and Charles L. P. Silet, eds. *The Pretend Indians: Images of Native Americans in the Movies*. Ames: Iowa State University Press, 1980.

Beale, Calvin. "Migration Patterns of Minorities in the United States." *American Journal of Agricultural Economics* 55 (1973): 938–46.

Bean, Lowell J. "Cahuilla." In *Handbook of North American Indians*, ed. William C. Sturtevant. Vol. 8, *California*, ed. Robert F. Helzer, 575–87. Washington, D.C.: Smithsonian Institution, 1978.

———. *Mukat's People: The Cahuilla Indians of Southern California*. Paperback ed. Berkeley: University of California Press, 1974.

———. "Power and its Applications." In *Native Californians: A Theoretical Retrospective*, ed. Lowell J. Bean and Thomas C. Blackburn, 407–20. Ramona, Calif.: Ballena Press, 1976.

Bean, Lowell J., and Thomas C. Blackburn, eds. *Native Californians: A Theoretical Retrospective*. Ramona, Calif.: Ballena Press, 1976.

Bean, Lowell J., and Florence C. Shipek. "Luiseño." In *Handbook of North American Indians*, ed. William C. Sturtevant. Vol. 8, *California*, ed. Robert F. Heizer, 550–63. Washington, D.C.: Smithsonian Institution, 1978.

Bean, Lowell J., and Charles R. Smith. "Cupeño." In *Handbook of North American Indians*, ed. William C. Sturtevant. Vol. 8, *California*, ed. Robert F. Heizer, 588–91. Washington, D.C.: Smithsonian Institution, 1978.

Bean, Lowell J., and Sylvia Brakke Vane. "Cults and Their Transformations." In *Handbook of North American Indians*, ed. William C. Sturtevant. Vol. 8, *California*, ed. Robert F. Heizer, 662–72. Washington, D.C.: Smithsonian Institution, 1978.

Belle Highwalking. *Belle Highwalking: The Narrative of a Northern Cheyenne Woman*. Edited by Katherine M. Weist. Billings: Montana Council for Indian Education, 1982.

Benedict, Ruth. *Patterns of Culture*. New York: New American Library, Mentor Books, 1958.

Berger, Peter L., and Thomas Luckmann. *The Social Construction of Reality: A Treatise on the Sociology of Knowledge*. Garden City, N.Y.: Doubleday and Co., Anchor Books, 1967.

Berkhofer, Robert F., Jr. *The White Man's Indian*. New York: Alfred A. Knopf, 1978.

Blackburn, Thomas. "Ceremonial Integration and Social Interaction in Aboriginal California." In *Native Californians: A Theoretical Retrospective*, ed. Lowell J. Bean and Thomas C. Blackburn, 225–44. Ramona, Calif.: Ballena Press, 1976.

Briggs, Jean L. *Never in Anger: Portrait of an Eskimo Family*. Cambridge: Harvard University Press, 1970.

Bright, William, and Jane Hill. "The Linguistic History of the Cupeño." In *Studies in Southwestern Linguistics*, ed. Dell Hymes, with William E. Bittle. The Hague: Mouton, 1967.

Campbell, Maria. *Halfbreed*. 1973. Reprint. Lincoln: University of Nebraska Press, 1982.

Carrico, Richard. "The Struggle for American Indian Self-Determination in San Diego County." *Journal of California and Great Basin Anthropology* 1, no. 2 (1980): 199–213.

Castillo, Edward D. "The Impact of Euro-American Exploration and Settlement." In *Handbook of North American Indians*, ed. William C. Sturtevant. Vol. 8, *California*, ed. Robert F. Heizer, 99–127. Washington, D.C.: Smithsonian Institution, 1978.

Chapman, Abraham, ed. *Literature of American Indians: Views and Interpretations*. New York: American Library, 1975.

Chudacoff, Howard. *The Evolution of American Urban Society*. Englewood Cliffs, N.J.: Prentice Hall, 1975.

Clifford, James. "Introduction: Partial Truths." In *Writing Culture: The Poetics and Politics of Ethnography*, ed. James Clifford and George E. Marcus. 1–26. Berkeley: University of California Press, 1986.

————. "On Ethnographic Allegory." In *Writing Culture: The Poetics and Politics of Ethnography*, ed. James Clifford and George E. Marcus. 98–121. Berkeley: Univesity of California Press, 1986.

————. *Writing Culture: The Poetics and Politics of Ethnography*, ed. James Clifford and George E. Marcus. Berkeley: University of California Press, 1986.

Coffer, William E. "Genocide of the California Indians with a Comparative Study of Other Minorities." *Indian Historian* 10 (Spring 1977): 8–15.

Cohen, Ronald. "Ethnicity: Problem and Focus in Anthropology." *Annual Review of Anthropology* 7 (1978): 379–403.

Cohler, Bertram J., and Henry U. Grunebaum. *Mothers, Grandmothers, and Daughters: Personality and Child Care in Three-Generation Families*. New York: John Wiley and Sons, 1981.

Colleoni, Father Xavier. Personal interview. Pala, Calif. October 18, 1989.

Condello, Tracie. Personal interviews. Huntington Park, Calif. Jan. 28, Feb. 1, Feb. 8, Feb. 21, and May 4, 1989.

Cook, Sherburne F. "Historical Demography." In *Handbook of North American Indians*, ed. William C. Sturtevant. Vol. 8, *California*, ed. Robert F. Heizer, 91–98. Washington, D.C.: Smithsonian Institution, 1978.

————. "Migration and Urbanization of the Indians in California." In *The California Indians: A Source Book*, ed. Robert F. Heizer and M. A. Whipple. Berkeley: University of California Press, 1971.

————. *The Conflict between the California Indian and White Civilization*. Berkeley: University of California Press, 1976.

————. *The Population of the California Indians, 1769–1970*. Berkeley: University of California Press, 1976.

Costo, Rupert, and Jeanette Henry. *The Missions of Califor-nia: A Legacy of Genocide*. San Francisco: Indian Histo-rian Press, 1987.

Cuero, Delfina. *The Autobiography of Delfina Cuero, As Told to Florence C. Shipek*. Banning, Calif. (Morongo Indian Reservation): Malki Museum Press, 1970.

Dart, John. "American Indians Becoming More Open to Christian Worship Services." *Los Angeles Times*, March 25, 1989, Part I-A, 1, 5.

Dawn, Anna. Personal interviews. Huntington Park, Calif. Nov. 12, Nov. 16, 1988; Jan. 11, Jan. 18, Jan. 28, Feb. 1, Feb. 8, Feb. 22, April 26, and May 4, 1989.

Du Bois, Constance. "A Diegeño Fiesta at Mesa Grande." In *Some Last Century Accounts of the Indians of Southern California*, ed. Robert F. Heizer, Ramona, Calif.: Ballena Press, 1976.

Duby, Georges. "Ideologies in Social History." In *Construct-ing the Past: Essays in Historical Method*, ed. Jacques Le Goff and Pierre Nora, 151–65. Cambridge: Cambridge University Press, 1985.

Erdrich, Louise. *Love Medicine*. New York: Holt, Rinehart, and Winston, 1984.

Ethnic Groups in Los Angeles: Quality of Life Indicators. Los Angeles: University of California, Los Angeles, Ethnic Centers, 1987.

Faye, Paul Louis. "Christmas Fiestas of the Cupeño." *Ameri-can Anthropologist* 30, no. 4 (1928): 651–58.

Fischer, Michael M. J. "Ethnicity and the Post-Modern Arts of Memory." In *Writing Culture: The Poetics and Politics of Ethnography*, ed. James Clifford and George E. Marcus. Berkeley: University of California Press, 1986.

Fiske, Shirley J. "Urban Institutions: A Reappraisal from Los Angeles." *Urban Anthropology* 8 (1979): 149–71.

Forbes, Jack D. "The Native American Experience in Califor-nia History." *California Historical Quarterly* 50 (1971): 234–42.

Frank, Geyla. "Finding the Common Denominator: A Phe-nomenological Critique of Life History Method." *Ethos* 7, no. 1 (Spring 1979): 68–94.

Freeman, L. *Who Is Sylvia?* New York: Arbor House, 1979.

Friday, Nancy. *My Mother/Myself*. New York: Delacorte, 1977.

Geertz, Clifford. *Local Knowledge: Further Essays in Inter-pretive Anthropology*. New York: Basic Books, 1983.

―――. "The Struggle for the Real." *Islam Observed: Reli-gious Development in Morocco and Indonesia*, 90–117. New Haven: Yale University Press, 1968.

―――. "Thick Description: Toward an Interpretive Theory

of Culture." *The Interpretation of Cultures*, 3–30. New York: Basic Books, 1973.

Georges, Robert. "Toward an Understanding of Storytelling Events." *Journal of American Folklore* 82 (1969): 313–28.

Graves, Theodore. "Drinking and Drunkenness among Urban Indians." In *The American Indian in Urban Society*, ed. Jack O. Waddell and O. Michael Watson, 174–311. Boston: Little, Brown, and Co., 1971.

Green, Rayna. *Native American Women: A Contextual Bibliography*. Bloomington: Indiana University Press, 1983.

Gridley, Marion E. *American Indian Women*. New York: Hawthorn Books, 1974.

Guillemin, Jeanne. *Urban Renegades: The Cultural Strategy of American Indians*. New York: Cambridge University Press, 1975.

Hammer, S. *Daughters and Mothers, Mothers and Daughters*. New York: Quadrangle Press, 1975.

Hanson, Jeffrey, and Linda P. Rouse. "Dimensions of Native American Stereotyping." *American Indian Culture and Research Journal* 11, no. 4 (1987): 33–58.

Hanson, Wynne. "The Urban Indian Woman and Her Family." *Social Casework* 61, no. 8 (Oct. 1980): 476–83.

Harrington, John P. "Fieldwork among the Indians of California." *Smithsonian Institution Publication 3213*, 85–88. Washington, D.C.: Smithsonian Institution, 1932.

—————, ed. *A New Original Version of Boscana's Historical Account of the San Juan Capistrano Indians of Southern California*. Smithsonian Miscellaneous Collections 92.4. Washington, D.C.: Smithsonian Institution, 1934.

Harvey, Herbert R. "The Luiseño: Analysis of Change in Patterns of Land Tenure and Social Structure." *California Indians II*, 97–206. New York: Garland Publishing, 1974.

Heizer, Robert F. "Natural Forces and Native World View." In *Handbook of North American Indians*, ed. William C. Sturtevant. Vol. 8, *California*, ed. Robert F. Heizer, 649–53. Washington, D.C.: Smithsonian Institution, 1978.

Henretta, James A. "The Study of Social Mobility: Ideological Assumptions and Conceptual Bias." *Labor History* 18 (1977): 165–78.

Hertzberg, Hazel W. *The Search for an American Indian Identity: Modern Pan-Indian Movements*. New York: Syracuse University Press, 1971.

Heth, Charlotte, Professor of Ethnomusicology, UCLA. Telephone conference, April 24, 1990.

Hill, Jane H., and Rosinda Nolasquez, eds. *Mulu'Wetam: The First People, Cupeño Oral History and Language*.

Banning, Calif. (Morongo Indian Reservation): Malki Museum Press, 1973.

Hodge, William H. "Navajo Urban Migration: An Analysis from the Perspective of the Family." In *The American Indian in Urban Society*, ed. Jack O. Waddell and O. Michael Watson, 346–92. Boston: Little, Brown, and Co., 1971.

Hoxie, Frederick E. *A Final Promise: The Campaign to Assimilate the Indians, 1880–1920*. Lincoln: University of Nebraska Press, 1984.

Hultkrantz, Åke. *The Religions of the American Indians*. Berkeley: University of California Press, 1967.

Jackson, Helen H. *A Century of Dishonor: A Sketch of the United States Government's Dealings with Some of the Indian Tribes*. 1881. Reprint. Minneapolis: Ross and Hairnes, 1964.

———. *Ramona*. Boston: Roberts Brothers, 1884.

Jackson, Helen H., and Abbot Kinney. *Report on the Condition and Needs of the Mission Indians of California, Made by Special Agents Helen Jackson and Abbot Kinney to the Commissioner of Indian Affairs*. Washington, D.C.: Government Printing Office, 1883.

Jorgensen, Joseph G. "The Indians and the Metropolis." In *The American Indian in Urban Society*, ed. Jack O. Waddell and O. Michael Watson, 66–113. Boston: Little, Brown, and Co., 1971.

Kelley, Jane Holden. *Yaqui Women: Contemporary Life Histories*. Lincoln: University of Nebraska Press, 1978.

Kelsey, C. E. "Report of Special Agent for California Indians to the Commissioner of Indian Affairs, 1906." In *Federal Concern about Conditions of California Indians, 1853–1913: Eight Documents*, ed. Robert F. Heizer. Socorro, N.M.: Ballena Press, 1979.

Kornhaber, Arthur, and Kenneth Woodward. *Grandparents, Grandchildren: The Vital Connection*. Garden City, N.Y.: Doubleday, Anchor Press, 1981.

Kroeber, Alfred. *Handbook of the Indians of California*. Smithsonian Institution Bureau of Ethnology Bulletin 78. Washington, D.C.: Government Printing office, 1925.

Kroeber, Theodora. *Ishi in Two Worlds: A Biography of the Last Wild Indian in North America*. Berkeley: University of California Press, 1961.

Kroeber, Theodora, and Robert F. Heizer. *Almost Ancestors: The First Californians*. San Francisco: Sierra Club, 1968.

Langness, L. L., and Geyla Frank. *Lives: An Anthropological Approach to Biography*. Novato, Calif.: Chandler and Sharp Publishers, 1981.

Larsen, David. "The Invisible Minority." *Los Angeles Times,* Oct. 8, 1989, Part VI, 1, 12–13.

Lee, Dorothy. *Freedom and Culture.* Englewood Cliffs, N.J.: Prentice Hall, 1959.

Le Goff, Jacques, and Pierre Nora. *Constructing the Past: Essays in Historical Methodology.* Cambridge: Cambridge University Press, 1985.

Lincoln, Kenneth. *Native American Renaissance.* Berkeley: University of California Press, 1983.

Longfish, George C. "Contemporary Native American Art." Exhibition. Stillwater: Oklahoma State University, Gardiner Gallery, Oct. 1–28, 1983.

Lothrop, Gloria Ricci. "*El Viejo:* Serrian Context." *The Californians* (Nov.–Dec. 1989): 16–27.

Lummis, Charles F. "The Exiles of Cupa." *Out West* 16, no. 5 (May 1902): 465–79.

———. "Turning a New Leaf." *Out West* 18, no. 4 (April 1903): 441–55, 589–602.

Lurie, Nancy O. "The Enduring Indian." *Natural History Magazine* 75, no. 9 (Nov. 1966): 10–22.

Margolin, Malcolm. *The Way We Lived: California Indian Reminiscences, Stories, and Songs.* Berkeley: Heyday Books, 1981.

Miller, Dorothy. "Alternative Paradigms Available for Research on American Indian Families," 79–100. *The American Indian Family: Strengths and Stresses.* Proceedings of the Conference on Research Issues, Phoenix, Ariz., 1980.

Momaday, N. Scott. "The Man Made of Words." In *Literature of the American Indians: Views and Interpretations,* ed. Abraham Chapman, 96–110. New York: New American Library, 1975.

———. *The Names: A Memoir.* New York: Harper and Row, Publishers, 1976.

Monkkonen, Eric. "Residential Mobility in England and the United States, 1850–1900." *Themes in British and American History: A Comparative Approach, c. 1760–1970.* Milton Keynes, England: Open University Press, n.d.

Moses, L. G., and Raymond Wilson, *American Indian Lives: Essays on Nineteenth- and Twentieth-Century American Indian Leaders.* Albuquerque: University of New Mexico Press, 1985.

Mountain Wolf Woman. *Mountain Wolf Woman, Sister of Crashing Thunder: The Autobiography of a Winnebago Indian.* Edited by Nancy O. Lurie. Ann Arbor: University of Michigan Press, 1961.

Native American Research Group. *Native American So-*

cialization to Urban Life: Final Report. San Francisco: Institute for Scientific Analysis, a Division of Scientific Analysis Corp., n.d.

Neisser, E. *Mothers and Daughters: A Lifelong Relationship*. Rev. ed. New York: Harper and Row, 1973.

Ortiz, Simon J. "Survival This Way." *A Good Journey*, 28. Tucson: Sun Tracks and University of Arizona Press, 1984.

Pearce, Roy Harvey. *Savagism and Civilization: A Study of the Indian and the American Mind*. Berkeley: University of California Press, 1988. Rev. ed. of *The Savages of America*, 1953.

Phillips, George H. *Chiefs and Challengers: Indian Resistance and Cooperation in Southern California*. Berkeley: University of California Press, 1975.

————. *The Enduring Struggle: Indians in California History*. San Francisco: Boyd and Frazer Publishing Co., 1981.

Powers, Stephen. *Tribes of California*. Berkeley: University of California Press, 1976.

Price, John A. "The Migration and Adaptation of American Indians to Los Angeles." *Human Organization* 27 (1968): 168–75.

Prucha, Francis Paul. *The Great Father: The United States Government and the American Indians*. Lincoln: University of Nebraska Press, 1986.

Purdue, Bill. "Urban Values and Rural Values." *Themes in British and American History: A Comparative Approach, c. 1760–1970*. Milton Keynes, England: Open University Press, n.d.

Qoyawayma, Polingaysi (Elizabeth White). *No Turning Back*. Edited by Vada F. Carlson. Albuquerque: University of New Mexico Press, 1964.

Rawls, James L. *Indians in California: The Changing Image*. Norman: University of Oklahoma Press, 1984.

Red Horse, John G. "American Indian Elders: Unifiers of Indian Families." *Social Casework* 61, no. 8 (Oct. 1980): 490–93.

————. "American Indian Families: Research Perspectives," 1–12. In *The American Indian Family: Strengths and Stresses*. Proceedings of the Conference on Research Issues, Phoenix, Ariz., 1980.

————. "Family Structure and Value Orientation in American Indians." *Social Casework* 61, no. 8 (Oct. 1980): 462–67.

Red Horse, John G., Ronald Lewis, Marvin Felt, and James Decker. "Family Behavior of Urban American Indians." *Social Casework* 59, no. 6 (Feb. 1978): 67–72.

Rigdon, Susan M. *The Culture Facade: The Work of Oscar Lewis*. Urbana: University of Chicago Press, 1988.

Robertson, J. "Grandmotherhood: A Study of Role Conception." *Journal of Marriage and Family* 39 (1977): 165–74.

Robinson, John A. "Personal Narratives Reconsidered." *Journal of American Folklore* 94, no. 371 (1981): 58–85.

Rolle, Andrew. *California: A History*. 4th ed. Arlington Heights, Ill.: Harlan Davidson, 1987.

Ryan, Patricia. Personal interviews. Huntington Park, Calif. Dec. 3, 1988; Jan. 14, Feb. 15, April 26, and May 4, 1989.

Ryan, Robert A. "Strengths of the American Indian Family: State of the Art," 25–43. In *The American Indian Family: Strengths and Stresses*. Proceedings of the Conference on Research Issues, Phoenix, Ariz., 1980.

Sekaquaptewa, Helen. *Me and Mine: The Story of Helen Sekaquaptewa*. Edited by Louise Udall. Tucson: University of Arizona Press, 1969.

Shankman, Paul. "The Thick and the Thin: On the Interpretive Theoretical Program of Clifford Geertz." *Current Anthropology* 25, no. 3 (June 1984): 261–78.

Shaw, Bruce. "Life History Writing in Anthropology: A Methodological Review." *Mankind* 12, no. 3 (June 1980): 226–33.

Shipek, Florence Connolly. "History of Southern California Mission Indians." In *Handbook of North American Indians*, ed. William C. Sturtevant. Vol. 8, *California*, ed. Robert F. Heizer, 610–18. Washington, D.C.: Smithsonian Institution, 1978.

————. *Pushed into the Rocks: Southern California Land Tenure, 1769–1986*. Lincoln: University of Nebraska Press, 1987.

Shoemaker, Nancy. "Urban Indians and Ethnic Choices: American Indian Organizations in Minneapolis, 1920–1950." *Western Historical Quarterly* 19, no. 4 (Nov. 1988): 431–47.

Silko, Leslie Marmon. *Storyteller*. New York: Seaver Books. 1981.

Simmons, James L. "One Little, Two Little, Three Little Indians: Counting American Indians in Urban Society." *Human Organization* 36 (1977): 76–79.

Simpson, George E., and J. Milton Yinger. *American Indians and American Life*. New York: Russell and Russell, 1975.

Simross, Lynn. "The Plight of Native Americans on the 'Urban Reservation.'" *Los Angeles Times*, April 16, 1986, Part V, 1, 4.

Slagle, Allogan. "Review Article." *American Indian Quarterly* 16, no. 1 (1992): 75–81.

Snipp, C. Matthew. "On the Costs of Being an American Indian: Ethnic Identity and Economic Opportunity." In *Proceedings of the Conference on Comparative Ethnicity: Ethnic Dilemmas in Comparative Perspectives*, ed. James H. Johnson, Jr., and Melvin Oliver. Los Angeles: University of California Institute for Social Science Research, June 1–3, 1988.

Sorkin, Alan L. *The Urban Indian*. Lexington, Mass.: Lexington Books, 1978.

A Statistical Profile of the American Indian, Eskimo, and Aleut Populations for the United States: 1980. Washington, D.C.: Racial Statistics Branch, Population Division, Bureau of Census, September 1985.

Stauss, Joseph H., and Bruce A. Chadwick. "Urban Indian Adjustment." *American Indian Culture and Research Journal* 3 (1979): 23–38.

Stedman, Raymond William. *Shadows of the Indian: Stereotypes in American Culture*. Norman: University of Oklahoma Press, 1982.

Stewart, James H. "Urbanization, Peoplehood, and Modes of Identity: Native Americans in Cities." *Selected Proceedings of the First and Second Annual Conference on Minority Studies* 1 (1975): 107–36.

Strong, William D. *Aboriginal Society in Southern California*. Banning, Calif. (Morongo Indian Reservation): Malki Museum Press, 1987.

Sutton, Imre. "A Selected Bibliography of the California Indian, with Emphasis on the Past Decade." *American Indian Culture and Research Journal* 12, no. 2 (1988): 81–113.

Swann, Brian, and Arnold Krupat. *I Tell You Now: Autobiographical Essays by Native American Writers*. Lincoln: University of Nebraska Press, 1987.

Talamantez, Inéz M. "Use of Dialogue in the Reinterpretation of American Indian Religious Traditions: A Case Study." *American Indian Culture and Research Journal* 9, no. 2 (1985): 33–48.

Tax, Sol. "The Impact of Urbanization on American Indians." *Annals of Political and Social Science* 436 (1978): 121–36.

Tedlock, Dennis. *The Spoken Word and the Work of Interpretation*. Philadelphia: University of Pennsylvania Press, 1983.

Thornton, Russell. *American Indian Holocaust and Survival: A Population History since 1492*. Norman: University of Oklahoma Press, 1987.

Thornton, Russell, Gary D. Sandefur, and Harold G. Grasmick. *The Urbanization of American Indians: A Critical Bibliography*. Bloomington: Indiana University Press, 1982.

Titon, Jeff Tod. "The Life Story." *Journal of American Folklore* 93, no. 369 (1980): 276–92.

Tönnies, Ferdinand. *Gemeinschaft und Gesellschaft: Grundbegriffe der Reinen Soziologie*. 8th rev. ed. Leipzig: Buske, 1935.

Trafzer, Clifford E., ed. *American Indian Identity: Today's Changing Perspectives*. Sacramento, Calif.: Sierra Oaks Publishing Co., 1985.

Underhill, Ruth. "Religion among American Indians." In *American Indians and American Life*, ed. George E. Simpson and J. Milton Yinger, 127–36. New York: Russell and Russell, 1975.

Vogt, Evon Z. "The Acculturation of American Indians." In *American Indians and American Life*, ed. George E. Simpson and J. Milton Yinger, 137–46. New York: Russell and Russell, 1975.

Wagner, Jean K. "An Examination and Description of Acculturation of Selected Individual American Indian Women in an Urban Area." Ph.D. diss., New York University, 1972.

————. "The Role of Intermarriage in the Acculturation of Selected Urban American Indian Women." *Anthropologica* 18 (1976): 215–29.

Wallace, Grant. "The Exiles of Cupa." *Out West* 19, no. 1 (July 1903): 25–41.

Weibel, Joan Crofut. "Native Americans in Los Angeles: A Cross-Cultural Comparison of Assistance Patterns in an Urban Environment." Ph.D. diss., University of California, Los Angeles, 1977.

Weibel-Orlando, Joan. *Indian Country, L.A.: Maintaining Ethnic Community in Complex Society*. Urbana: University of Illinois Press, 1991.

————. *Urban American Elders Outreach Project Final Report*. Los Angeles County Area Agency on Aging, Department of Community and Senior Citizens Services, 1989.

Yancey, William L., Eugene P. Ericksen, and Richard N. Juliani. "Emergent Ethnicity: A Review and Reformulation." *American Sociological Review* 41 (June 1976): 391–403.

Yarger, Sister Mary. Personal interview. Pala, Calif. Oct. 18, 1989.

White, Raymond C. "The Luiseño Theory of 'Knowledge.'" *American Anthropologist* 59 (1957): 1–19.

———. "Religion and its Role among the Luiseño." In *Native Californians: A Theoretical Retrospective*, ed. Bean and Blackburn, 355–77. Ramona, Calif.: Ballena Press, 1976.

———. "Two Surviving Luiseño Indian Ceremonies." *American Anthropologist* 55, no. 4 (1953): 569–78.

Zunz, Oliver. *The Changing Face of Inequality*. Chicago: University of Chicago Press, 1982.

INDEX

Garra, Antonio, 42, 157n.38

Harvey, J. Downey, 44
Healing, 117–18
Helm, Anna May Lawson Smith: basketweaving, 18; birth, 27, 81; death, 133; divining, 139; education, 27; employment, 53; illness, 87; religion (*see* Chapter 5); residency, 27, 53, 60
Helm, Mary Place, 27
Helm, Steven, 11, 12; and alcohol, 60; attachment to homelands, 50; burial at Pechanga, 51; marriage, 27; religion, 114–15. *See also* Chapter 5
Helm, Turner, 27
Hemet, Calif., 98
Huntington, Park, Calif., 3, 7, 31, 52, 60, 99, 129, 152

Indian Free Clinic, 7, 97
Indian Mental Health Clinic, 59
Indianness, 4, 6–8, 10–19, 21–23, 27, 55, 57, 62, 98, 100, 105, 148, 149, 154n.23. *See also* Culture, change/persistence of; Ethnicity; Pan-Indianism
Indians:
    Cahuilla: communities, 11, 37–42 (*see also* Pala; Wilakalpa); language, 38; missionization, 33, 36; world view, 39, 63, 65, 66, 102, 105, 106, 112, 120, 123, 124, 130, 135, 161n.22
    California, 4, 11, 12, 17, 33–42, 54, 61, 62, 94, 111–13, 116–17, 126, 142, 143, 163nn.16, 7. *See also* Indians: Cahuilla, Cupeño, Diegeño, Mission, Serrano
    Cupeño: Christianization, 125–29; communities, 11, 42 (*see also* Agua Caliente; Cupa; Pala; Wilakalpa); culture, 66, 141–43, 148–50; language, 38, 148; missionization, 33, 36; removal, 43–50, 164n.28; world view, 39, 65, 66, 81, 107, 112, 150
    Diegeño (Kumeyaay), 33, 34, 36, 37, 38
    Luiseño: communities, 11, 37, 42, 51 (*see also* Pala; Pechanga; Wilakalpa); language, 38; missionization, 33, 36; world view, 39, 65, 66, 103, 116, 124, 135, 165n.44
    Mission, 4, 17, 33–36, 42, 53, 54, 111, 126, 143. *See also* Indians: California
    Navajo, 61, 62, 148

Plains, 15, 143
Serrano, 33
Sioux, 61–62
Indians, images of, 9, 155n.36. *See also* Stereotype
Intermarriage, 7, 21, 22, 155n.43
Interrelatedness. *See* Reciprocity
Interviews, 5, 19, 24

Jealousy, 80
Jimsonweed. See *Toloache*
Julian, Calif., 51

Kearney, Stephen Watts, 42
King, Belva May Helm: attachment to homelands, 51;
    birth, 28, 81; death, 134; education, 28; employment,
    14, 29, 58; religion, 115 (*see also* Chapter 5)
King, Charles, 23, 28, 85–87
King, Charles, Jr., 18, 28
Kinship, 12, 20, 22, 23, 24, 81–89, 94, 95, 100–101,
    145, 162n.7. *See also* Family

Lake Elsinore, Calif., 51
La Leyenda Blanca, 35, 156n.7
La Leyenda Negra, 35, 156n.7
Las Vegas, Nev., 137, 138, 147
Lawson, Louise, 81
Life history, 4, 5, 20, 149, 155n.39
Long Beach, Calif., 54, 60
Los Angeles, Calif., city of, 6, 14, 15, 17, 20, 28, 29, 31,
    52, 54, 55, 57, 60, 105, 106, 127, 140, 151, 158n.77,
    159nn.79, 81, 82, 162n.7, 163n.12
Los Angeles, Calif., county of, 14, 57
Luiseño Indians. *See* Indians, Luiseño
Lummis, Charles, 42–50
Lynwood, Calif., 31

Mentalité, 21–23, 25–26, 62, 68–70, 77, 80, 88, 89, 94,
    105–107, 143–46, 154n.23, 160n.4
Mesa Grande, Calif. (Mesa Grande Indian Reservation),
    11, 14, 28, 126
Metaphysics, 20, 25. *See also* Chapter 5
Mission Indians. *See* Indians, Mission
Missionization, 33–36, 40, 125